Fixing the Racial Wealth Gap:

Racism & Discrimination Put Us Here, But This Is How We Can Save Future Generations

Fixing the Racial Wealth Gap:

Racism & Discrimination Put Us Here, But This Is How We Can Save Future Generations

Rodney A. Brooks

August Press
Suffolk Virginia

*"For Mattie B. Brooks, my mom, and my inspiration.
Thank you for believing in me."*

FIXING THE RACIAL WEALTH GAP

Copyright 2021 by Rodney A. Brooks. All rights reserved.

Published in the United States of America. No part of this book may be used in any manner whatsoever without written permission, except in the case of brief quotations embodied in critical articles or reviews.

For more information contact August Press, 941 Vineyard Place, Unit D, Suffolk, VA 23435 or wdawk69643@aol.com

Cover illustration by R. Alan Brooks
Rodney Brooks photo by Washington Post

ISBN 978-0-9791686-2-8
First Edition

10 9 8 7 6 5 4 3 2 1

Table of Contents

Foreword 7
Introduction 11

01	How we got here: A brief history of economic racism in the United States	14
02	Closing the Back-White Wealth Gap	24
03	How to find a financial planner.........................	36
04	The importance of creating a budget	40
05	This is why you need an emergency fund	48
06	The ABCs of saving and investing	55
07	The power (and the danger) of becoming a 401(k) millionaire	70
08	How to decide when you should take Social Security	76
09	How credit scores worsen the wealth gap	82
10	The estate plan: A key to generational wealth	89
11	Understanding insurance and the role in played in creating the wealth gap	99
12	Financial literacy is a key to growing generational wealth	110
13	Black women face unique financial challenges............	118
14	What if you haven't saved enough for retirement?........	127
15	Don't let your kids (or other family members) ruin your finances	139
16	Is starting a business part of your financial plan? It may be harder than you thought	147
17	Marriage, divorce and communications	156
18	Are reparations part of a solution?.....................	163
19	Fixing the wealth gap: Some real strategies	169

Index 177
Financial Planning Resource Guide 197
Acknowledgements 207
Notes 208

Foreword

In the midst of a national conversation about race in which conservatives are mainly arguing that it is wrong to teach kids about "critical race theory" because it might cause emotional distress for white kids, it is noteworthy that the explanatory power of critical race theory—which is an academic analytical framework that assesses how racism has influenced the politics, policies and practices in institutions and systems throughout the U.S.—withstands scrutiny across many areas of American life including the cause and effect of the racial wealth gap.

The racial wealth gap—in which the typical African American household (at the time of this writing) owns approximately one nickel of wealth for every dollar owned by the typical White household—illustrates the yawning chasm between the economic status of African Americans and Whites as measured by their wealth, or the amount of material assets they own minus what they may owe.

If a broader understanding of the racial history of the U.S. including it atrocities were outlawed, which is the goal of conservatives, it would be natural for Americans of all racial and ethnic backgrounds to assume that the personal financial behaviors of African Americans is the cause of the racial wealth gap. Messages like: "You would be much better off financially if you wouldn't have bought X, Y, or Z (insert purchase of choice: "Cadillac" "shoes" "clothing") would be the standard explanation given for the gap by whites and blacks alike.

But because we have insight into the modern underpinnings of the racial wealth gap, as well as the historical context, we know better than to blame individuals within racial groups for their economic circumstances.

For example, a study conducted by researchers at Brandeis University followed the same households over a twenty five year period and found that the gap between similarly situated White and African American families nearly tripled, increasing from $85,000 in 1984 to $236,500 in 2009.

They discovered that the largest drivers for the growth in the racial wealth gap over time were policy shaping factors that resulted in more advantages for whites in their homeownership, employment and educational experiences followed by more white advantages in family inheritances and other family financial supports. They also found that marriage created a significant wealth boosting effect for white couples but had no similar effect for African American couples. When compared to the drivers above, the individual financial behaviors of blacks had a minimal effect on the racial wealth gap.

These study results should not be surprising given that we also know that U.S. policies and practices have proactively worked to boost the wealth of white Americans throughout its history. From slavery, which allowed white families and institutions to accumulate wealth on the backs of unpaid black laborers, and the Homestead Act, which gave government subsidized free land to whites only, to the initial implementation of the Social Security Act, which left out 65 percent of the black workforce at its passage in 1935 by excluding payments for domestic and agricultural workers, and a plethora of real estate laws and practices that restricted advantageous housing opportunities for African Americans by limiting the places where they could live and undercutting their borrowing opportunities, the history of U.S. policies is literally an encyclopedia of methods U.S. governments at every level have used to exclude or marginalize black households. Thus, it is public policy, which is the spoils of politics, that is largely responsible for creating and sustaining the racial wealth gap in the United States of America.

That being said, the ability of individuals to better manage their finances and make smarter financial investments remains a necessary imperative for all people, but especially for people born into historically marginalized racial and ethnic group households without solid wealth accumulation and management experiences. Too many of these individuals have not had the benefit of learning, in school or through their families, how to manage and accumulate money and other lucrative assets through business ownership, homeownership, and investing in equities among other asset building activities.

Because there are real and often dire consequences for the wealth gap as lived by these households—larger instances of indebtedness, higher rates of poverty, fewer assets to rely on in financial emergencies, greater housing insecurity—any factor that can help build better economic security is important.

That is why this book by Rodney A. Brooks is timely and necessary. A journalist extraordinaire who has had a long and productive career reporting on the serious economic issues facing vulnerable households while also possessing direct and successful experience with important asset building strategies such as home- and business ownership, Rodney is perfectly positioned to provide guidance that will help people from economically insecure backgrounds build and sustain wealth.

And the urgency of his book cannot be understated. I've been studying, implementing advocacy strategies, and leading efforts to educate policymakers about why it is important to close the racial wealth gap since the early aughts. When I first started down this path, the typical African Americans household owned twelve cents for every dollar of wealth owned by the typical white family.

Unfortunately, the positioning of black households has dramatically declined over the span of the two decades I've been working on this issue. This is a direct result of the housing crisis that enabled wealth stripping of black households on a grand scale and the global financial crisis of 2008 that caused greater unemployment and an accelerated loss of homeownership among African American families. And now, still not recovered from these events, African American households have been devastated by the global COVID-19 pandemic which has had a gross and disproportionately negative impact on employment, businesses ownership, and the health and life expectancies of people of color.

Our nation is at its zero moment and so are many low wealth households. Rodney Brooks brings us a piece of the solution with this vital work.

Dr. Maya Rockeymoore Cummings
Founder, President & CEO
Global Policy Institute

Introduction

I've spent most of my life as a financial journalist. I've also served as an informal financial advisor to many of my African American friends and colleagues of over the years. And I've become passionate about financial literacy.

Whenever a new employee walked in the door, I would make sure that they were signed up for the company 401(k). I would pull them aside and explain the free money thing – when a company matches your contributions (as most companies do) to a retirement plan and you aren't signed up, you are passing up free money.

I got so frustrated with a veteran reporter who was married with young children who never signed up for his 401(k) that I literally walked him up to the HR department and turned him over to the benefits administrator.

I grew frustrated with the human resources department that would only give new employees an 800 number and tell them to call in to get signed up for their 401(k) that I complained to the publisher that the company was not giving young employees any guidance on something that could have a huge impact on their lives.

The point is that like me, many of these young people, and some of older ones, were not taught about finances and investments. Even if they signed up, they had to pick investments on their own.

That's not something we are taught in school and, unlike some of my White colleagues, that's not something we discussed over the dinner table. That's not blame our parents, because they struggled to just work and take care of their families.

My parents didn't have the financial knowledge and they didn't own stocks, but they set me up with the values and motivation that helped me achieve success. They scraped together the money to buy our first home and move to the suburbs, where I was able to get a better education that would prepare me for college. My father died at 43, when I was 16 years old. My mother, with 16 and 14-year-old boys still at home, didn't have the money to pay tuition, but she pushed me and motivated me to apply to college. And she helped to support me emotionally and financially (when she could) through my four years of college. This book is a tribute to her.

My initial intention was to write a financial planning guide that was specifically aimed at Black Americans and the unique problems we face as a race – the racial wealth gap, the income gap, discrimination in housing and education and health disparities.

There are real reasons why the wealth gap is so wide. A report from the Federal Reserve Bank in Minneapolis said that there has been zero progress in closing the wealth gap for the last 70 years. A report by Prosperity Now and the Institute of Policy Studies says the net worth of Black Americans would be zero by 2053 if current trends continue.

As helpful as a financial planning guide for Black Americans would be, it would be remiss on my point to offer financial advice without some significant discussion about why we are in such a dire economic condition.

Since slavery the federal government, state governments, banks and other institutions have maintained a system of racism and discrimination that has prevented us from developing generational wealth. Often, through the years, when we did acquire wealth, we were robbed of it by angry White mobs or the very institutions and governments that were supposed to protect us.

States had laws that prohibited White Americans from even teaching us to read.

It's critically important that before we talk about financial literacy the wealth gap and why Black folks can't save or build wealth, that we understand all the depressing reasons why and the impact they have had on us over generations.

History isn't taught in schools the way it was when I was a student in the 1960s. And Black history was certainly not taught. Much of what I learned, I learned from library books and, later in college Black history classes. Still, politicians are determined to Whitewash that history for our future generations.

That's why I begin this book with the documented racism, discrimination and atrocities committed against Black people over the last 400 years. Only if you understand the reasons we are where we are can you begin to understand why it is so important to keep our future generations from falling victim to the same lack of understanding of money and finance that we have had to endure for so long.

Rodney A. Brooks

01

How we got here: A brief history of economic racism in the United States

CHAPTER 01

Black Americans have lived under the shadow of state-sanctioned racism for 400 years. The institution of slavery was followed by institutionalized discrimination; massacres and riots in cities across the nation, both big and small, including Tulsa (Oklahoma,) Rosewood (Florida), New York and Philadelphia, lynchings, land theft, Jim Crow laws, "sundown towns," which banned Blacks entirely; redlining in housing, and the killing of unarmed Black men and women by police officers. All of those racist acts have been endorsed and institutionalized by federal, state and municipal governments and even the judicial system.

The result is that we are suffering economic distress. We earn less than White Americans, even at the same levels of education. We save less because we earn less. We leave our children and grandchildren with nothing because we die with nothing. Single Black women, 60 years and older with a bachelor's degree, have a median net worth of about $11,000, according to William Darity and A. Kirsten Mullen in their book From Here to Equality, while single White women with a college degree in the same age range have a median net worth of $384,000.

Talk to a Black funeral home director. They deal in cash because often Black families come to them with no money to bury their dead. We literally have to pass the hat among family members just to bury our parents.

How did the racial wealth gap grow so wide? Our history is filled with broken promises, legal injustices and systematic racism and discrimination. If you really think about it, we are only 150 years removed from slavery. The enslaved were freed but were given no means of survival. It's a real wonder that our descendants survived at all.

"It's been about the policy and practice of the United States of America," said Maya Rockeymoore Cummings, the widow of Rep. Elijah Cummings and CEO of Global Policy Solutions in Washington, D.C. "People of African heritage were enslaved in this country and prevented from earning wages off their own labor. In fact, the rewards of it went to White families and to White organizations, institutions and ultimately to our nation.

"African people basically built the agricultural backbone of this country," she said. "And yet, they were prevented by law from actually being rewarded with the wealth of their labor. We built the wealth of this nation and its institutions and have perpetually over time been prevented from reaping the rewards."

Forty Acres and a Mule

The federal government promised forty acres and a mule to the formerly enslaved multiple times after the Civil War. It was an empty promise. After President Abraham Lincoln was assassinated, President Andrew Johnson proceeded to dismantle the program. Meanwhile, 1.5 million White settlers were given 160-acre land grants.

"Even after slavery, when there was an opportunity to repair the wrongs of slavery, the Freedmen's Bureau tried to establish a robust system of programming that would help African Americans in the areas of education, banking and economic security," said Rockeymoore Cummings. "There was active White hostility to that agenda. There was an organized effort to basically undermine the Freedmen's Bureau and basically undo the compensatory structure of the post slavery reconstruction."

Tulsa and other race riots

"If we look back historically, going back to the Black Wall Street era, anytime we started accumulating some type of wealth, especially coming out of the era of slavery going into reconstruction, those towns and those businesses were decimated," said Nick Abrams, a Certified Financial Planner and president of AJW Financial Partners in Baltimore, Maryland. "And we've had to start over and over again, which has limited our ability to create that generational wealth."

Massacres and riots like those in New York, Philadelphia, Atlanta, Houston, Detroit and dozens of other American cities since the 1900's were aimed at stripping Black Americans of the wealth they had accumulated. Black lives, Black wealth and Black businesses were all destroyed in these violent racial clashes instigated by angry and jealous White Americans. Economist and author Julianne Malveaux tells the story of a Black man, Anthony Crawford, who had accumulated more than 400 acres of land in Georgia, only to be lynched and have his property stolen by Whites.

Willa and Charles Bruce purchased land in Manhattan Beach, California in 1912 and built a Black resort, Bruce's Beach, to serve Black residents. Because of segregation it was one of the few beaches that Black residents could use. But 12 years later the city seized the land and forced them from their property. Repeatedly in American history Blacks were murdered, chased out of town and stripped of their wealth and property.

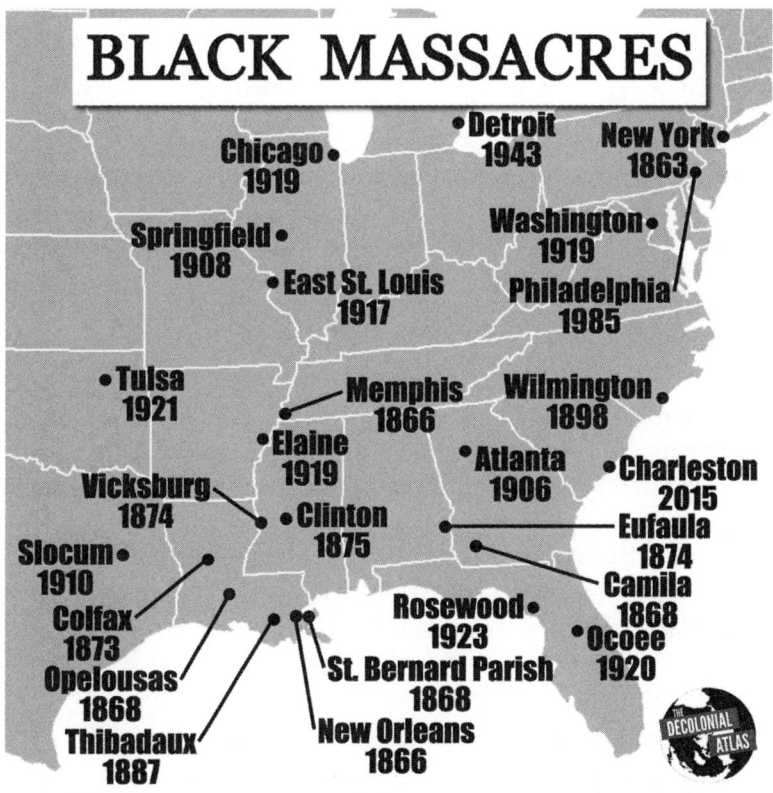

Black Massacres in the US. Map by Jordan Engel

In 1951 a group called the Civil Rights Congress submitted a paper named We Charge Genocide to the United Nations Genocide Convention accusing the United States of genocide. The 200+ page report charged that "the oppressed Negro citizens of the United States, segregated, discriminated against, and long the target of violence, suffer from genocide as the result of the consistent, conscious, unified policies of every branch of government."

The report described 152 incidents in which unarmed Black men and women were killed and hundreds of other acts of violence were committed by police or White mobs between 1945 and 1951. W.E.B. DuBois was one of the signees. Copies mailed to the U.N. in Paris never arrived, presumably confiscated by the U.S. government. Activist and singer/actor Paul Robeson delivered the paper to the U.N., but after a member of the CRC personally delivered a copy to the Genocide Convention in Paris, his passport was revoked. The U.S. press mostly ignored it, but it got attention in the international press. The U.N. never acknowledged receipt of the petition, presumably because of the influence of the United States government.[1]

USDA's racist policies devastated Black farmers

Black farmers were denied assistance from the USDA, which also played an active role in bankrupting Black farmers, literally, since its inception. Black farmers ultimately won $1.25 billion in a discrimination settlement against the USDA in 2010, but it was far too late. Black farmers made up 14 percent of the U.S. farming population in 1910. Today they account for just 1.4 percent. "We have lived under economic terrorism for decades," one Georgia farmer, who's land was in foreclosure because of the USDA's racist policies, told NBC News in 2020.[2]

The Great Depression and the New Deal

Prior to the Great Depression, Black unemployment was routinely double or triple that of Whites. But after the stock market crashed in 1929, the low paying jobs that had been available to Blacks were filled by Whites. Black unemployment in 1932 was a whopping 50 percent. Unemployment rates among Blacks in the South were routinely double or triple that of Whites, said historian Cheryl Lyn Greenberg in her book "To Ask for an Equal Chance: African Americans in the Great Depression." Atlanta had a Black unemployment rate of nearly 70 percent in 1934; the rate was 60 percent in Philadelphia and Detroit and 50 percent in Chicago and Pittsburgh. Meanwhile, the White unemployment rate was 25 percent in many cities across the north.

Social Security

The law prevented Black families from receiving it because it was initially designed to keep out agricultural or domestic workers, and at the time that it passed in 1935, 65% of African Americans were in agricultural and domestic labor jobs.

Black World War II veterans were denied the same benefits as White veterans

The wide disparity in the implementation of the GI Bill was a major driver in wealth, income and education gaps between Black and White Americans. While the GI Bill's language did not specifically exclude African Americans, it was structured in a way that offered little or no assistance to Black veterans. For example, racist White politicians pushed the implementation of the law down to the state level, where racist Southern states did all they could to make sure Black veterans could not benefit. For example, Levittown, Pa., offered the dream of home ownership to thousands of returning veterans with the assistance of the Federal Housing Authority and U.S. Veterans Administration. But the developers, with the blessings of those federal agencies, still refused to sell homes to Blacks and, in fact, wrote racial covenants into each deed.

Redlining and housing discrimination

There were so many racist policies in the real estate industry that it's just about impossible to discuss them all. In the 1930s the federal government along with banks and other lenders created city maps to determine where they would lend money to people buying homes. Black inner-city neighborhoods were most likely to be outlined in red. Banks refused to lend money to buy or even improve homes in those areas.

Now keep in mind that discrimination and racist laws also kept Black Americans from moving out of those areas to buy homes. A study by researchers at the National Community Reinvestment Coalition, the University of Wisconsin – Milwaukee and the University of Richmond found that "the history of redlining, segregation and disinvestment reduced Black wealth, but also impacted health and longevity."

This is significant because a huge portion of Black wealth resides in housing. The inability to invest in an appreciating asset puts strict limits on that wealth. In addition, it has been proven that White home appraisers significantly undervalue homes owned by Blacks even when they are in White neighborhoods.

One Black couple in California got an appraisal that they thought considerably undervalued their home. They removed all traces that a Black family lived there and replaced family photos with those of a White family. Their new appraisal came in a half million dollars[3] above the first one.

Racism and discrimination in education

The United States has a long history of outright racism when it came to educating Blacks. States made it illegal to teach Blacks, even free Blacks, and people like Margaret Crittenden Douglass[4] were actually imprisoned for doing so in Virginia in 1849. Blacks were forced to go to schools established by Quakers and Christians to get an education. But turmoil and violence directed towards these White educators forced these schools to close.[5]

State and federal courts upheld racial segregation multiple times before Brown vs. the Board of Education. The "separate but equal" doctrine was ingrained in the Plessey vs. Ferguson court ruling. "In the area of education, it was felt that the children of former slaves would be better served if they attended their own schools and in their own communities."[6]

It wasn't until 1954 that the U.S. Supreme Court outlawed racial segregation in public schools in the landmark Brown vs. the Board of Education in Topeka. Americans often forget that as late as the 1960s most African American, Latino, and Native American students were educated in wholly segregated schools funded at rates many times lower than those serving Whites and were excluded from many higher education institutions entirely.[7]

Throughout history institutional racism has created an invisible chain holding down students of color in the educational system. Limitations and denial of access to education created a culture where students of color were treated as less than equals, a mindset that is still deeply rooted in our educational system today.[8]

When a federal judge ordered schools in Prince Edward County, Virginia to integrate, the county voted in 1959 to shut down rather than integrate. The school board used tuition grants to open schools for White children. Black children, meanwhile, were shut out of county schools for five years. Quaker groups and local churches established private schools for Black children until the U.S. Supreme Court ordered Prince Edward County to reopen in 1964.

This deep-rooted racism in education has impacted the ability of Black men and women to earn a decent wage.

"In the United States, wealth and education already feed into each other in an intergenerational cycle, according to a report from the Center for American Progress. "Families with more wealth are able to provide more educational opportunities for their children, who are in turn able to capitalize on those opportunities in ways that create more wealth. This reinforcement of wealth through education and of education through wealth—when combined with the racially disparate economic and health impacts of the COVID-19 pandemic—will only further widen existing racial wealth and education gaps. The intergenerational transmission of racial wealth inequality is playing out at rapid speed during the pandemic.[9]"

Racism and discrimination at hospitals

There is a centuries-old record of racial discrimination in the U.S. health care system. During the 1918 influenza epidemic, which killed 675,000 Americans and 500 million people worldwide, Black communities, already crippled by poverty, Jim Crow segregation and rampant discrimination, were mostly forced to rely on family members for care.

While Black Americans were less likely to catch the disease (likely because of segregation), they were more likely to die if they did catch it. Unless they lived in one of the few urban centers like Washington, D.C., Chicago or New York City where they had Black hospitals they were relegated to substandard care in the basement of segregated hospitals, or, more likely, turned away altogether.

CHAPTER 01

When Medicare threatened to withhold federal funding from any hospital that practiced racial discrimination, under the Civil Rights Act of 1964, hospitals desegregated almost overnight.

Before the passage of Medicare and Medicaid the healthcare system was tightly segregated. Hospitals in the South complied with Jim Crow laws, excluding Blacks from hospitals reserved for Whites or providing basement accommodations for them. Many Black communities in the South had basically no access to hospitals. Most of the Black births in Mississippi were at home, which has a huge impact on infant and maternal mortality among Blacks.[10]

When America catches the flu

There's an old saying, 'When America catches the flu, Black people catch pneumonia." A friend in North Carolina says their old saying is even stronger: 'When White America catches the flu, Black people die.'

Yes, it's dramatic, but historically true. Throughout history Black Americans have suffered worst financially during an economic downturn. And before we can recover, we are hit again, harder. The Black unemployment rate is consistently twice that of the White unemployment rate, and the Center for American Progress says that gap is built into the labor market. The Great Recession hit Black Americans with such force and impact that we still have not recovered more than a decade later.

- The Great Depression (1933-1940). U.S. unemployment peaked at 25 percent in 1933 and remained above 14 percent until 1940. Black American unemployment was double or triple White Americans during this decade. "Prior to the Great Depression, African Americans worked primarily in unskilled jobs. After the stock market crash of 1929, those entry-level, low-paying jobs either disappeared or were filled by Whites in need of employment. According to the Library of Congress, the African-American unemployment rate in 1932 climbed to approximately 50 percent.[11]"
- The Great Recession (2008-2009). In 2009 the White unemployment rate was about 9 percent, while the

unemployment rate for Black Americans was 16 percent. The home foreclosure crisis wiped out 54 percent of Black wealth, while White household net worth dropped by 17 percent.[12]

- The COVID-19 pandemic. The pandemic had a disproportionately harmful impact on communities of color. Hardest hit were jobs in the service industry, which were held predominantly by Black and Hispanic workers. Some estimates were that 40 percent of Black businesses shut their doors during the pandemic. Most were not expected to come back.

"We have to focus in a massive way on eradicating racism, so we're not so grossly impacted by all of this," says Roland Martin, political commentator and host of the digital Roland Martin Unfiltered. "It just speaks to the inequities all around. When it comes to African Americans in every facet of their lives, it's like a domino.

There's one thing, and then there's another and another and another. And the bad hits just keep on coming."

This history is not here to depress you or anger you. It is here to lay the basis for how complicated and deep the history of racism is for Black America and how that and oppression played in the racial wealth gap.

We'll spend the rest of the book talking about the issues and real solutions to boosting wealth among Black Americans.

The crippling racial wealth divide has plagued Black America for centuries. That portends a grim outlook, especially as we prepare to retire.

02

Closing the racial wealth gap

CHAPTER 02

"We are using all of our money to maintain life," says Rene Nourse, a certified financial planner (CFP) and CEO of Urban Wealth Management in El Segundo, California. "Some of us don't have extra money to build up worth."

The many inter-related issues indicate a major and long-lasting economic crisis facing African Americans.

- **Income and wealth disparities.** The net worth of the average White family is $171,000, nearly ten times greater than that of a Black family's $17,150, according to a 2016 Brookings Institution report. And though Black Americans make up 13 percent of the nation's population, their share of the nation's wealth is only 2.5 percent, said William Darity, professor of public policy at Duke University.
- **Historically low home ownership.** Home ownership is the chief source of wealth for many Americans, but only 43% of Black people own homes, compared with 72% of White people.
- **Low savings rates and a lack of participation in the stock market.** Just 34% of African Americans participate in retirement savings plans, while 60% of Whites do, according to the Federal Reserve.
- **Low or no investment in stocks.** Only 33% of Black households owned stocks in 2019, while nearly 61% of White households did. Less than half of people of color who responded to an Allianz Life survey said they own investments and other accounts that can help with retirement security, including life insurance, Individual Retirement Accounts and annuities.
- **Heavy dependence on Social Security benefits for retirement income.** Retired Black Americans depend heavily on Social Security. Those who don't save enough for retirement often come to rely on Social Security. "According to the U.S. Social Security Administration, about 38% of minority beneficiaries rely on Social Security for 90% or more of their income, compared with 28% percent of White

people. Social Security benefits can be lower for African Americans because benefits are based on income and Black workers have historically earned less.

- **Lack of legacy planning and generational wealth.** One big reason high- and middle-income White families are so much wealthier that Black families of similar age and income is inheritances. Economists William A. Darity and Darrick Hamilton say inheritances "account for more of the racial wealth gap than any other demographic and socioeconomic indicators."

Income and wealth disparities

The net worth of the average White families is $171,000, nearly ten times greater than that of a Black family's $17,150, according to a 2016 Brookings Institution report.[13] And though Black Americans make up 13 percent of the nation's population, their share of the nation's wealth is only 2.5 percent, said William Darity, professor of public policy at Duke University.

The Center for Retirement Research[14] at Boston College found a huge racial gap between the retirement readiness of White Americans and minorities. And a report from Allianz Life found that retirement readiness may be at risk for people of color, who tended to overestimate their retirement preparedness. "Oftentimes in communities of color, breadwinners are expected to balance support for multiple generations with their personal retirement goals. This complexity, among others, could be responsible for the disconnect we see between perception and reality, putting People of Color at higher risk for retirement insecurity," said Cecilia Stanton Adams, Allianz Chief Diversity and Inclusion Officer.

"We have to first understand root causes," says Eric Bailey, CEO of Bailey Wealth Advisors in Silver Spring, Maryland. "That traces back centuries. Even today we are paid less than our counterparts for the same job. That creates disparity out of the gate because you have less discretionary income. Without discretionary income, it becomes difficult for people to save and accumulate wealth."

Solutions to closing that wealth gap range from increased financial education, increasing the number of African American financial advisors to much more complicated solutions like baby bonds and slavery reparations.

Historically low home ownership rates

A report from real estate brokerage Redfin found that only 44% of Black families owned their homes as of the first quarter of 2020, compared with 73.7% of White households, based on an U.S. Census Bureau data.

Black home ownership peaked around 2008, and then the housing crisis and Great Recession of 2009-2009 hit. Black households faced foreclosure at twice the rate of their White neighbors, largely because they were targeted with subprime loans. Since they were hurt more than other communities, it will take them longer that others to recover. By most standards, the Black community has not recovered, more than a decade later.

Black homeownership hit a record low of 40.6% in the second quarter of 2019. The number increased to 47% for the second quarter of 2020, but Census Bureau data shows that Black Americans still have the lowest rate of homeownership among all U.S. racial groups. During the Great Recession, Black and Latino households, many of whom lived in neighborhoods that were ravaged by foreclosures or steep housing price declines, suffered devastating losses of household wealth, and they still haven't caught up. For low-income renters of all races and ethnicities, housing cost burdens have soared in recent years, despite a strong economy.[15] In fact, all gains in Black home ownership since the Fair Housing Act have been erased.

The coronavirus pandemic made things even worse. "People of color and low-income families were already facing crushing housing cost burdens and housing instability, stemming in large part from structural racism and a long history of discriminatory housing and lending practices. Last year, a larger share of Black and Latino renters had difficulty paying rent than White households, and the homeownership gap between Black and White families reached record highs.[16]

The Urban Institute found that not one city among the 100 U.S. cities with the largest number of Black households is anywhere near closing the Black and White homeownership gap. In Minneapolis, which faced widespread civil unrest following the death of George Floyd, the homeownership gap is 50% between White and Black residents. Even in cities with larger Black populations and more economic opportunity, like Washington, D.C. and Los Angeles, a large homeownership gap of 20 to 25% remains, the report said.[17]

Low savings rates and little participation in the stock market

Only 33.5% of Black households owned stocks in 2019, according to the Federal Reserve. Among White households, the ownership rate is nearly 61%. African Americans don't trust the system and are not willing to risk their assets, because many do not have enough wealth to take financial risks.

"We developed a lack of trust in the system early on along with us not having financial education in the community," said Financial Advisor Eric Bailey of Bailey Wealth Advisors in Silver Spring, Maryland. "We are not being taught. It's not a conversation our kids see us having around the table. It's not a conversation happening with families."

Nourse says Black women are especially hurt by the wealth inequities. Many times, women have to put careers on hold when they start a family. "We're raising kids and tend to be responsible for taking care of our elders. And because of income inequality, we are not making enough money to focus on our future."

Estate planning and generational wealth

White families are twice as likely to receive an inheritance as Black families, and that inheritance is three times as large.

Most Black businesses don't survive past the first generation. Financial tools like reverse mortgages are wreaking havoc on the transfer of homes to younger generations and Black Americans are notoriously underinsured when it comes to life insurance.

Certified Financial Planner Nicholas Abrams of Baltimore says the lack of insurance is a big negative. "Stop buying $25,000 in life insurance, just enough to put you in the ground," he says. "Leave some money to your family so they can take it and grow it and leave money to following generations. We can't build wealth with each generation starting from scratch. We have to do a better job of leaving money and leaving legacies."

One report estimates that 80 percent of Black Americans die without a will, and that is probably overly generous. Look at the Black entertainers who died without a will – Prince and Aretha Franklin among them. Their estates are still in probate. The average probate process can last six to nine months, depending on the state. And that's with an estate plan.

Property taxes

For decades, White tax assessors placed a heavier tax burden on Black residents by intentionally overvaluing their property. In the Jim Crow South, officials used property taxes to punish Black homeowners and churches that boycotted White businesses or hosted civil rights meetings.

Several recent studies and investigations show that, racially motivated or not, many tax assessors still routinely saddle Black and minority residents with property tax bills that are too high given the value of their homes.[18]

In 2017, the *Chicago Tribune* published a series of stories on the Cook County Tax Assessor's Office, finding that for years the county's property tax system had given huge financial breaks to homeowners in wealthier and largely White communities while placing an unfair burden on poorer people living in minority communities.

A 2018 investigation by the Philadelphia Inquirer and the Philadelphia Daily News found that homes in the city that sold for between $25,000 and $50,000 were assessed 70 percent higher than they should have been. The tax bill on a $37,500 home was inflated by about $360 a year.

Meanwhile, owners of homes that sold for $1 to $2 million were assessed at nearly 11 percent below their true value. Tax bills on those homes were $2,000 less than they should have been.

MIT researchers found that Black Americans pay $743 more annually than White Americans when it comes to mortgage interest payments, $550 more per year in mortgage insurance premiums and $390 more each year in property taxes — totaling more than $13,000 over the life of the loan. the inequities totaled to $67,320 in lost retirement savings for Black homeowners.

Financial planners

A significant factor in the financial well-being of Black Americans may be a lack of professional help. Only 32% of those surveyed said that they are working with a financial professional.

We need to get more Blacks into the financial planning professions. Many Black Americans are uncomfortable talking to anyone about their finances, but they would be more comfortable talking to a Black financial planner. But the numbers of Blacks in the profession are atrocious. According to the CFP Board there were only 1,355 Black Certified Financial Planners (CFP) in 2019, up 8 percent from the previous year.

Finding solutions

Money, investing, stocks and bonds... these are not discussions we have at the family dinner table. But they should be taking place. That's one thing Black Americans need to fix.

- We need to promote financial literacy in schools. Personal finance classes need to be a part of the regular curriculum in middle and high schools. And we need to talk to our children about finances. Of course, that means that some parents need to be educated themselves. But there are classes, websites and seminars that can do that.

- We also must educate people about financial planners and the importance of things like financial plans and estate plans.
- African Americans need to create wealth through home ownership and by acquiring financial assets, including employer-sponsored retirement plans, and homes. Based on latest Federal Reserve data, only 34 percent of African Americans participate in retirement savings plans vs. 59.6 percent White participation.
- Finally, we need to pass generational wealth to our children and grandchildren. That means we need to work on estate planning and buy life insurance so we can leave assets to future generations.

Finding a financial planner

A Black financial planner told me a story about a client that I'll share with you. His client was a government employee who had saved and accumulated a nice nest egg in her government retirement accounts.

She wasn't poor by any means. She had worked virtually her entire career for the federal government and was ready to retire. She wanted to reward herself, so she raided her retirement account and paid cash for a brand-new BMW – without telling her financial advisor.

Here's the problem. She couldn't afford it. She had saved several hundred thousand dollars for retirement, but a $40,000 cash withdrawal would put her retirement in jeopardy. Besides Social Security, this money needed to last her for the rest of her life. And, as a woman, it would likely be a long life. She was robbing her future self of thousands of dollars in future growth and dividends that would support her later in life. In addition, she forgot about taxes. Money invested in 401(k)s are tax-deferred, not tax free. She was going to get hit with a whopping tax bill the next year.

Oh, and it gets worse. By pulling $40,000 out of her retirement accounts she was increasing her gross income for that year. Say, she retired at the end of the year and earned $80,000 in salary. She effectively raised her income to $120,000 that year with the withdrawal.

CHAPTER 02

Lucky for her, her financial planner convinced her to take the car back.

She was one of the lucky ones. She was smart enough to hire a CFP even though she intentionally didn't tell him about the BMW because she was afraid that he would talk her out of it. The story had a happy ending.

But she, like millions of other Americans, are faced with the most money they've ever had in their lives when they retire. It looks like a lot of cash until you realize that it has to last you for the rest of your life. Social Security is not going to be a lot of help. The average Social Security payment is only about $1,543 a month, or $18,516 a year.

People can do stupid things when they come into a lot of money. Think of all the multimillion-dollar lottery winners who've gone bankrupt in a few short years. Or athletes who sign big contracts and spend it quickly, not really thinking about how short their careers are. The average career of an NFL player is only 2 ½ years, 4.8 years for an NBA player and 5.8 years for an MLB player.

But back to the importance of having someone help you make your financial decisions. My family did not have discussions about finances around the dinner table or under any other circumstances as I was growing up. I didn't have a checking account until I went away to college, so I knew nothing about how to balance it. Many Black families don't talk about money. We have to figure it out as we go through life.

"Wisdom is something we acquire as we get older," one 60-something Black woman told me in an interview. "If I had only known about things that transpired, I would have done a lot of things differently."

A recent Allianz Life study found that retirement readiness may be at risk for people of color, who tended to overestimate their retirement preparedness. A separate report from the Center for Retirement Research at Boston College found a huge racial gap between the retirement readiness of White Americans and minorities.

A significant factor in the retirement readiness of minorities may be a lack of professional help, Allianz says. A CNBC poll found that 99 percent of Americans don't use a financial advisor.[19] But most of those who do work with a financial advisor have less fears about running out of money in retirement and are more secure about surviving a recession.

What's the difference between a CFP® and other financial planners?

There are more than 200 different designations for financial professionals. And the truth is that anyone can call themselves a financial planner or financial advisor, whether they have training or not. Here are some of the top designations.

Certified Financial Planner (CFP)®
This is one the most widely recognized and respected credentials in financial planning. Candidates must have a bachelor's degree and complete college or university-level coursework through a CFP Board Registered Program. Required coursework general principles of financial planning; education planning; insurance planning; investment planning; tax planning; retirement savings and income planning; and estate planning. Upon completion of the coursework, students must then take a board exam – two sessions lasting three hours each. Professional experience and continuing education are also required.

Chartered Financial Analyst (CFA)
A professional designation given by the CFA Institute. The designation measures and certifies the competence and integrity of financial analysts. Candidates must have completed a four-year college or university degree, or they must have at least four years of professional work experience. They must also pass three exams.

Chartered Life Underwriter (CLU)
This is a professional designation for those who wish to specialize in life insurance and estate planners. It requires five core courses in insurance planning, individual life insurance, life insurance law, estate planning and planning for business owners and professionals.

Chartered Financial Consultant (ChFC)
This professional designation comes after the completion of a comprehensive course that includes financial education, examinations and practical experience. The eight required courses are financial planning, insurance planning, income taxation, retirement planning, investments, estate planning, personal financial planning, and contemporary applications in financial planning.

One of the reasons the CFP® is so highly regarded is that financial planners with that designation are held to a strict standard of fiduciary duty. That means they are required to put the interests of their clients before their own. That means they are forbidden to buy products for their clients strictly to get a commission or to simply push their company's products when they are not in the best interest of their clients.

When you should start with a professional financial planner

Virtually every financial planner I have ever talked to has stories about people coming in for their first visit when it's too late. Some have already turned in their retirement papers to their jobs. Others are in their early 60s and ready to retire in the next few months.

They can tell you it's never too late to hire a financial planner, but months before retirement is too late. It's a very difficult conversation to tell someone he or she can't retire because they have not saved enough money. I once talked to a guy who was 38 and about to retire. The problem was that he only had $40,000 in his 401(k). That's crazy. He was determined and he didn't listen. I lost track of him so I can't tell you how things ended up for him.

Here's a good rule of thumb. Life gets in the way. You are establishing yourself in your 20s, and often marriage and home ownership come in your 30s. That's a good time to start talking to a financial advisor. You are going to be facing hard decisions about savings, investments, retirement planning and planning for college tuition. But that doesn't mean you should wait until then to contribute to your 401(k). You should begin those contributions with your first job. Most employer-sponsored 401(k)s have a company match, and when you don't contribute, you are walking away from free money.

This is not to discourage you from seeing a financial planner in your 50s. It still makes sense and there's still time. A financial planner can make a difference in 10 or 15 years. It's imperative that you figure out how much you are spending and when it makes sense to retire.

Most financial planners will also work with you to determine the best time to take Social Security for you and your spouse. The ultimate verdict may be that you must work a few more years or find a part-time job for a few years. But you are greatly increasing the odds that you will not run out of money in retirement.

Eric Bailey, founder of Bailey Wealth Advisors in Silver Spring, Maryland, says in the past the industry has not focused on Black financial advisors. Also, Blacks may be somewhat distrustful of financial advisors because some of the early ones were basically salespeople for the financial services industry trying to sell products to our community. Also, he said, some may feel that they don't have enough financial resources to interest a financial planner. "You probably should have a financial plan when you have less resources," he said.

03

How to find a financial advisor

Now that we know what to look for, the question is how to find one. There are online directories. For online help, the Financial Planning Association will help you find a financial planner. If you are specifically looking for a Black financial planner, look up the Association of African American Financial Advisors, which is based in Washington, D.C. But keep in mind that Blacks are grossly underrepresented in this field, for a variety of complicated reasons.

According to the CFP Board there were only 1,355 Black certified financial planners in 2019, up 8 percent from the previous year.

LeCount Davis is widely considered the dean of Black Financial planners. He is also considered the first Black CFP® when he received his certificate in 1987. He also founded the Association of African American Financial Advisors (AAAA) in 2001. Today, he is in his 80s and still active in the industry.

Eric Bailey, founder of Bailey Wealth Advisors, says only since 2005 has he started to see the number of Black CFP® increase in the mid-2000s. Before that the financial planners were mostly salespeople, many in the insurance industry.

Today, the major banks and brokerages have financial planners and financial advisors, but there is always the possibility that they will push you into investment products from their institutions.

I don't think there is anything wrong with getting advice from advisors with banks or brokerages. There are certainly benefits, like larger staffs and big research departments. But you should also consider an independent fee-only financial advisor. I have nothing against the one-person operations. There are some really smart one-person CFPs®. But frankly, I believe you should show a preference for the larger companies who have support staff.

Do your homework

Do some homework before you choose the advisor you're going to be working with. You can find much information online nowadays or ask friends and co-workers who they work with and if they're satisfied with that advisor's recommendations and level of service provided. Make sure you interview potential candidates to see who the best fit for you would be, which independent advisor will be able to provide the types of products and services you require, along with unbiased recommendations, and who you feel you would be able to build a long-lasting trust and relationship with.

Other than the directories from financial planning organizations, the best way to find a financial planner is through a personal reference. Get a list of at least three. Do your research on each, and then do a telephone interview. If they don't have time to talk to you on the phone, then cross them off the list.

This is a person that, hopefully, you will be working with for years, possibly for the rest of your life. You need to make sure both you and your spouse or partner is comfortable with your choice. Do an in-person interview. Go in with a list of your questions.

If the financial advisor talks over your head, that is a problem. It is also a problem if the financial planner talks down to you. If your financial advisor talks only to one spouse, that is a problem.

And don't assume that if a financial planner was perfect for your parents, the same one is good for you. You might feel better and more comfortable with someone closer to your age, or, if you're a woman, a financial advisor who is female. I've talked to financial advisors whose client base consisted mostly of divorced women. There are others whose base is almost completely people 60 and older, or Millennials.

Take your time and find the right fit. And if a year later you don't think it's working out, don't hesitate to take you money and move on. Remember, this person is working for you.

Some questions you should ask during the interview

1. Are you a fiduciary? Federal law requires that a fiduciary look out for your interests ahead of his or her company's. That means they

should not be selling you company branded products just to receive the commission.

2. Are you a Certified Financial Planner® or do you have another professional designation?

3. Who will be your contact? Will it be the person you are interviewing or a junior member of the staff?

4. Will the firm produce a personal financial plan for you?

5. How often will you meet to go over your financial plan? You should have an in-person meeting once or twice a year at the very minimum to review your portfolio's performance, your goals and your levels of risk. Much can happen in a year. Your marital status may change. You may have children, buy a house or a car or have teenagers starting college. Any or all of these can change your plan and how you budget.

6. Who will manage your portfolio? Will it be the person you are interviewing or a junior member of his staff?

7. If your financial advisor is a money or portfolio manager, but not a CFP®, is there a financial planner on the team.

8. How will they collect their fees for their services? This is really important. Some people have no idea how their financial advisors are paid or how much they are paid.

Fee-only vs, asset based

Several organizations, including the National Association of Personal Financial Advisors, recommend a fee-only advisor mainly because it is the most transparent. When it comes to financial planners selling you products for which they get a commission, there is an obvious possibility of a conflict of interest when it comes to the best interest of the clients – the reason the Obama Administration pushed through fiduciary rules which the Trump Administration later diluted. A true fiduciary is "required" to put the interest of his or her clients first. The fee-only financial advisors are paid hourly, through a retainer, a flat fee or as a percentage of your assets.

04

The importance of creating a budget

CHAPTER 04

Sixty-five percent of Americans have no idea of what they spent last month, according to a survey by Mint.com. Another survey says that 35 percent of Americans paid a bill late because they simply forgot about it.

Millennials seemed to be the least concerned about budgeting. Of those aged 18–24, only 23 percent reported knowing what they'd spent in the last month, the lowest of any age group. But nearly half of the Baby Boomers, those aged 55 and up, knew how much they'd spent in the previous month.

Still, 31 percent said they regretted how much they spent, and 44 percent of Americans say money, especially the lack of it, is a leading cause of their stress.

On the other hand, 62 percent of those who have a budget said they are less stressed and more confident about spending, according to the CFP Board, which sets and enforces standards for Certified Financial Planners®.

Two of the big reasons people say they don't budget is they don't have the time, or they don't need to budget. But another reason that should rank just as high is -- it's easy to just put it off.

We've already looked at some of the Black-White wealth gap numbers. Black family wealth is only one-tenth of that of White families. And only a third of Black Americans save in a workplace retirement plan vs. more than 60 percent of Whites. If nothing else, that data shows a big reason why Black Americans need to budget. There is no data that can tell you how many Black families use a monthly budget, but any financial planner will tell you a budget is critical to getting your financial house in order.

There is, however, plenty of data on how Black Americans spend. A Nielsen report, It's in the bag: Black consumers' path to purchase, found that Black Americans spend nearly $54 million on ethnic hair and beauty products and $62 million on men's toiletries. A few more highlights:[20]

- 52% of African Americans find physical shopping to be relaxing, 26 percent more that the total population.
- 55% say they like wandering the store, looking for new and interesting products. (Consumer buying experts say this is a good way to overspend or make purchases you did not plan).

- Black Americans have an affinity for high-end stores, especially Saks Fifth Avenue, Neiman Marcus and Bloomingdale's. "Black consumers are more likely than the total population to agree 'I am willing to pay extra for a product that is consistent with the image I want to convey.' They also buy $500 handbags and jewelry at a higher rate than the total population," the report said.

Theodore Daniels, a financial planner and founder and executive director of the Society for Financial Education and Professional Development (SFE&PD), says Black Americans need to focus on wealth building assets, like buying homes and investing in 401(k)s.

"As long as you stay away from those wealth building components, the wealth gap will never close," he said. "Personal use assets just decrease in value. There is a fork in the road. You can go to the left or right. To the right you can add to consumer spending or go to the left and start creating wealth for yourself and the community at large.

"When something goes wrong, we get impacted the most, Daniels added. "We have to look long term and not stop short-term spending."

A budget will help you get there

For Daniels and many other financial planners, the first thing they do with a client is to make them write down what they bring in in terms of income, and what goes out in expenses. Many surveys show us that the lack of a budget is one of the biggest financial planning mistakes people say they make before retirement. And retirees say their biggest mistakes were not saving enough and not having a budget.

When clients put their expenses on paper, they are often shocked. One financial planner says they are wrong 98 percent of the time, and they are usually way off. Many times, they spend twice as much in a month than they thought.

CHAPTER 04

Creating a budget

STEP 1
Gather your bills and statements.

The hardest part is the first step. It's the information gathering. Gather three to six months of your bank statements and credit cards statements. Six months is preferred. Look at what you are spending on and how often.

Next, gather your monthly bills – utilities, mortgage or rent, telephone, internet and cable, streaming services, car note.

Make sure you include expenses you may pay annually, like auto and home insurance, taxes, home security. And don't forget to include the costs for personal grooming the barber, hairdresser and nail salon, which could add a $100 or more to your monthly budget.

STEP 2
Put your expenses into categories, or buckets.

Financial planners generally want you to put your expenses into three categories or buckets: Your needs, your wants and your wishes. Another way to look at the three buckets would be to categorize them as your essentials, your niceties and your luxuries. This helps people segment what they pay for the basics. It's a key step for people close to retirement because they want to ensure that their basic living expenses are covered by their income, especially if they are on a fixed income.

- Your needs or essentials will include your basic living costs: your food, mortgage, car payment, transportation, utilities, health care, clothing. Health care expenses should include dental care and eye care.
- Your wants or niceties will be things like the weekend trips to restaurants, the summer vacation or the weekend trip to the beach.
- The luxuries are those high-expense items such as a beach house, a new car purchase or that diamond ring for your 25th anniversary.

Step 3
List your income and assets.

Gather your pay stubs and bank account, brokerage and 401(k), 403(b) and IRA statements.

If you aren't being guided by a financial planner, there are free budget worksheets available on the internet, including https://www.nerdwallet.com/article/finance/budget-worksheet. Also, today, most banks and credit unions categorize your expenses as you write checks or use your ATM cards. That should make it easy.

Step 4
Is there an income gap?

If your expenses are higher than your income, than you have a problem. You are living on credit. That means you need to cut expenses, at least to the level where they are equal to or less than your income. Hopefully, your income will exceed your expenses enough that you can set aside at least a few dollars a month for savings or investment. It doesn't matter if you can't save much. Even if it's $20 a week. Let's do a little math. Twenty dollars a week saved over 20 years at just 5 percent interest will net you $13,700 in 10 years or $36,000 over 20 years due to the power of compounding. If you are lucky enough to get a 10 percent return, that $20 a week would turn into $18,200 over 10 years and $65,000 over 20 years.

Cutting expenses. I'm not going to tell you to cut out everything like cable TV and visits to Starbucks like some of the budget experts tell you. I think it's a mistake to cut the little things that you love. Some people need that cup of gourmet coffee or tea in the morning. Some people live for sports, so cutting cable may make them unhappy. Don't make yourself miserable.

Look at the budget and look for ways to cut expenses.

Some possibilities.

Insurance. Did you ever email someone who still has an AOL address?

I'm not making fun of them, only trying to make a point. It's the same reason advertisers spend billions of dollars capturing the attention of young people. They are hoping they get into a habit of buying a product and never switch. There are a bunch of people who never stopped using the AOL email address.

It's the same with people who sign up for services and never explore others, things like a cell phone or cable provider, insurance company or health insurance company. They may never change, and thus never look to see if there is a cheaper alternative. And believe me, there are always cheaper alternatives.

Auto insurance. You may not have even thought about whether African Americans pay more for auto insurance than White Americans. The fact is, we do. A study by the Consumer Federation of America found that good drivers who live in Black neighborhoods are charged much more than drivers who live in White communities – 70 percent more for premiums, or an average of $438 per year more.

My wife and I were with the same auto insurance company for years. I found a better policy that was hundreds of dollars cheaper. My wife resisted the change because she was used to that company. We have switched four or five times since and each time we saved hundreds or thousands on our annual policies.

Mortgages. According to a study from The Massachusetts Institute of Technology, Black Americans pay more than any other group to own a home. That disparity contributes half of the $130,000 retirement savings gap between Blacks and Whites.

Black homeowners pay more in mortgage interest, mortgage insurance and property taxes than other homeowners, according to the MIT Golub Center for Finance and Policy. The differences in mortgage interest payments amount to $743 a year, mortgage insurance premiums come to $550 a year and property taxes are about $390 per year, which total about $13,464 a year over the life of the loan.

This amounts to $67,320 in lost retirement savings for Black homeowners. "These inequities make it impossible for Black households to build housing wealth at the same rate of White homeowners.

Economists and housing experts attribute the disparities to "risk-based mortgage pricing." "For historical reasons. Black homeowners on average have lower credit scores and lower down payments and are thus disproportionately disadvantaged by risk-based pricing, and yet, that is the pricing system that predominates today."

It's one reason why you should look into refinancing to a lower cost mortgage. Racial inequities may still come into play, but you should at least see if you can get a lower mortgage rates or if you still have to pay for mortgage insurance. You can save thousands.

Cable TV, cell phone and internet. Cable TV makes it extremely difficult to reduce the bills even though you have hundreds of channels that you don't watch. But they are losing millions of customers to streaming services. Compare cable prices and switch if you can find a lower package. Often you can get introductory packages at reduced prices. But if you are primarily using streaming services, here is a major bill you can reduce. But watch out. These streaming services like Netflix and Hulu and Disney can add up fast. You can find yourself paying cable-sized bills for streaming.

You can often find major reduction in your mobile phone provider, especially if you are a senior and AARP member. It will depend on your needs and how you use the service. You can also save by reducing the number of cable boxes. Some cable companies still require the boxes even if you have a cable ready TV.

I recently called to cancel a newspaper subscription and a satellite radio subscription. Both offered to continue my subscriptions at special promotional 50 percent discounts for a full year. Though my initial intent was to cancel both for various reasons, I ended up keeping both. The point here is that you won't lose anything by asking, and these companies would rather offer you a promotional discount rather than lose your business.

Every month is not the same. Your budget should reflect that. August may be the month you spend on back-to-school clothing and supplies. December means Christmas, and holiday spending. November means Thanksgiving, and maybe double your food budget. January may be a month you take that family vacation to Disneyland. Making any and all a part of your budget will help keep them off your credit card.

CHAPTER 04

Other expenses. One of the biggest surprises can be eating in restaurants. Look at those expenses carefully. If you eat out twice a week, you can maybe save by going out once a week.

Pay down credit card debt. We owe nearly $1 trillion to credit card companies, and the average household credit card balance remains too high, at $8,089, according to Wallethub.com. Both figures are also likely to rise as the economy reopens from the coronavirus pandemic.

Interest on credit card debt can be incredibly high. Wallethub.com says the average credit card rate is 17.87 percent for new offers and 14.58 percent for existing accounts. One way to begin reducing your debt is to throw those high interest cards in a drawer until you pay them down. It won't matter how high your interest is if you pay off the balance monthly.

Avoid payday loans. Payday lenders typically make a loan to borrowers that is due to be repaid at the next payday. It is considered a predatory loan with an average interest rate of nearly 400 percent if it's paid within two weeks. If the loan is not repaid in two weeks, and most are not, the rates can soar above 500 percent. Some states impose limits, but many do not. Users of the loans are also more likely to file for bankruptcy.

AARP. It's the leading advocate organization for people 50 and over. If you are over 50, don't hesitate to join. It's not even the in-store senior citizen discounts that are most attractive. Going with AARP co-branded homeowners' insurance, auto insurance and life insurance can literally save you thousands a year. The website also offers news and consumer tips for its target audience.

05

This is why you need an emergency fund

CHAPTER 05

Two-thirds of Americans at all income levels would have trouble coming up with $1,000 to cover an emergency, according to one survey. Three-quarters of those earning less than $50,000 and two-thirds of those earning between $50,000 and $100,000 would struggle to pay an unexpected $1,000 bill. And 38% of households making more than $100,000 say they wouldn't be able to come up with that $1,000.

The very nature of an emergency tells you it is something that is unexpected. And that usually comes with a cost. If you are caught off guard and without the financial means to weather that emergency, you could suffer financial consequences for years to come.

That's one reason an emergency fund should be a critical part of your household budget. You need to set aside those funds before you save for college tuition, before you start your regular saving and investing and before you max out your 401(k).

Basically, an emergency fund is just what it sounds like - a separate savings account that you have set aside for any emergency or disaster that comes your way. Because many people don't have emergency savings they are forced into alternatives like high-interest credit cards, payday loans and personal loans. But keep this in mind. The average payday loan has an average Annual Percentage Rate of 664% according to the Center for Responsible Lending. The average credit card rate is 17.4 percent.

I have a friend who pays off her credit card bill every month. She has excellent credit. Still, she got an offer for a new card at "great" interest rate of 17.5 percent. Credit card debt is what most financial planners call "bad debt." Yet nearly 20 percent of the people who couldn't handle a $1,000 emergency expense said they would put it on a credit card.

When that emergency pops up, without an emergency fund, none of the alternatives are good. You get hit with a furnace repair in the winter and alternatives are to freeze or put that $1,000 on a high-interest credit card. We've already talked about how high credit card interest is, and the average credit card debt. Another alternative is to raid your 401(k) or IRA. That's also if there is no loan provision you will be hit with both taxes and penalties. And please, don't even consider a payday loan.

Women are much less likely than men to have an emergency fund. Nearly 50 percent of women don't have enough for car repairs vs. 34 percent of men and 23 percent of women have less than $100 saved vs. 13 percent of men according to Bankrate.com.

One of the biggest financial emergencies would be the loss of a job. Financial planners tell clients they need six to nine months' salary to be prepared for a job loss. That is a big number and scares some people into doing nothing. If I have household income of $100,000 a year and my spouse and I have two young kids, I'm going to be hard pressed to have $50,000 to $75,000.

But that's not the kind of emergency fund we're talking about here. You need to be able to cover unforeseen emergencies that could cost $1,000 or more.

What exactly is an emergency fund?

Even if you're not ready to cover your expenses in the event of a job loss, you still need to be ready for financial emergencies. This will cover some of the everyday emergencies we face without having to put it on a high-interest credit card on take out a loan.

One year I had to replace my furnace in the winter and my air conditioning system and hot water heater in the summer. It was a bad year, and I certainly was not prepared. But I learned a valuable lesson.

A friend put off calling a plumber for a leak in his basement because initially he didn't have the money and then he didn't prioritize saving for the repair. He ended to paying many times as much when the pipe burst. He had to hire the plumber at the emergency weekend rate in addition to the hundreds of dollars flood damage in his basement.

Most people don't think about how much everyday medical and home repairs cost. Here's a look at just a few estimates.

Medical emergencies. An emergency visit to the doctor or the dentist will cost you, even if you have insurance. The average cost of an emergency root canal is about $1,000, according to NerdWallet.

What about prescriptions after an accident or sickness? And don't forget pets. Emergency visits to the Veterinarian visits, especially during an emergency, can cost as much as for a human.

Some Top Emergency Medical Expenses[23]

Root canal	$500 to $3,000
Dental Filling	$100 to $450
Crown	$500 to $3,000
Avg. dental visit	$290
Hospital ER visit	$1,300
Emergency Pet visit	$800 to $1,500

Source: Carecredit.com, GoodRx.com

Car expenses. We're still a nation of drivers and most people cannot live without their cars. For most people if their car breaks down, they are crippled. And for most, the cost of repairs will go on a credit card, if they have that much credit available.

Some top car repair expenses[24]

Air conditioner	$500
Brake Line	$1,000
Transmission	$4,000 to $5,000
Fuel Pump	$700 to $1,000
Hybrid car battery	$6,000
Engine repair	$7,000 to $10,000

Source: Car Repair estimates and auto repair costs, CarBrain.com

Major household repairs. Your homeowners' insurance may cover that leaky roof, but it is not likely to cover that furnace repair in the middle of winter when temperatures are freezing. Or that air conditioning repair on the hottest days of summer. It could be anything from the old refrigerator going out or the stove blowing up. Imagine the peace of mind if you know you have the money to pay for it tucked away.

According to the website Motley Fool you can expect to spend 1 percent to 4 percent of your home's value just for annual maintenance. For a $400,000 property, you're therefore looking at $4,000 to $16,000 per year. The age of your home is a big indicator of what your maintenance will be. Expect to pay the lower end of the range for newer homes and towards the top of that range for older homes.

The cost of some major home repairs[25]:

	Range	Average
Roof replacement	$2,000 to $10,000	Average, $7,500
Mold remediation		Average: $2,500
Heating/air repair	$250 to $550	
Heating/air replacement	$5,000 to $12,500	
Water line replacement		Average: $2,500
Water heater	$500 to $1,000	
Water damage	$1,100 to $5,000	Average: $3,000

Source: Seven expensive home repairs, Maurie Backman, Fool.com, December 22, 2019

The emergency fund needs to be in cash, easily assessable and separate from your other savings and investments. You don't want to have to go to the dentist for the root canal and have to sell 10 shares of stock to do that. You should not be worried about the interest on this money because you need it to be liquid. It's hard for anyone to recommend holding $10,000 or $20,000 in a bank savings account or a money market account that pays little or no interest, but you need to be able to get at these funds quickly.

Extended Auto warranties

They get a lot of commercial time on TV, especially late-night TV, being hawked by celebrities. The big question is, are they worth the money.

"The fact is, extended warranties are overpriced," says personal finance expert and radio talk show host Dave Ramsey. "That's the reason people sell them because they make a bundle on them in commissions. "I don't recommend buying extended warranties, ever. If you can't afford to repair your car, then you can't afford the car.[26]"

Ramsey says car buyers should instead create an emergency fund for their cars. If that money isn't needed for repairs, it can go toward the purchase of the next car.

Home warranties

A home warranty is not an insurance policy, but a service contract that covers repair and replacement costs for your home's systems and appliances when they break down from routine use. Whether you've lived in the same home for years or recently purchased the home of your dreams, a home warranty can protect you and your budget from unexpected costs. These aren't repairs that are generally covered by your homeowners policy.

Without a home warranty, you could spend hundreds or thousands of dollars repairing or replacing major appliances or systems. If you don't have money set aside for these expenses, a home warranty can more than pay for itself.

According to Bankrate, home warranties can cost $350 to $600 and are advised if you buy an older home or if you're selling your home. They are attractive to homebuyers. They aren't necessary for a new home because appliances would still be covered by the manufacturer's warranty.

How to save for your emergency fund

There are millions of ways to do this. The safe thing to do is to set aside a couple of thousand dollars a year, so your fund grows as your home ages. I have friends who set aside $10 or $20 a week in a bible or in a dresser draw, and then transfer it to a bank when it grows.

CHAPTER 05

There are several apps you can download and put on your phone to help you budget, save and invest. Mint.com is one of the best reviewed. But one really smart one is Acorns. Connect it to a debit or credit card, and each time you make a purchase, it rounds up to the nearest dollar and sets that money aside in an investment account. In other words, buy a cup every day at Starbucks and it costs $2.59, it will put aside 41 cents to an investment account.

06

The ABCs of saving and investing

CHAPTER 06

The wealth of a White household is nearly eight times that of the typical Black household ($188,200 vs. $24,100). White households account for 60 percent of the U.S. population but account for 84 percent of the nation's wealth. Black households, meanwhile, account for 13.4 percent of the U.S. population and hold just 4 percent of the nation's total household wealth.

We've already talked in detail about some of the reasons for the wide wealth disparities, especially the historical discrimination and racism. Those inequities have led to long-term damage to Black psyche and culture when it comes to wealth. Consider a few facts about Blacks and investing.

- As of 2020, Black families have a median household income of just over $41,000, whereas White families have a median household income of more than $70,000.
- In the last 15 years, Black homeownership rates have declined to levels not seen since the 1960s, when housing discrimination was legal. The homeownership rate for Black 35- to 44-year-olds fell from 45 percent in 1990 to 33 percent in 2015, half the level for Whites of the same age and lower than the Black homeownership rate in 1960.[28]
- Only 35.5 percent of Blacks invest in stocks, vs. 61 percent of Whites, according to the Federal Reserve.
- Renter's median net worth in 2017 was only $3,036 vs. homeowners' net worth of $269,000, according to the U.S. Census Bureau. That includes $160,100 in home equity and the remaining wealth was other investments like retirement accounts.

"From a savings standpoint, there's a mindset that has to change," said Nick Abrams, president of AJW Financial Partners in Baltimore, Maryland. "The mindset has to be pay yourself first. Whatever you earn, set aside a percentage of it to pay yourself by putting it in some type of an account whether it's to do your job with your own individual account."

"We can't be afraid to take risks," he said. "The news will have you believe that the stock market's going to crash every other day. But when we look at it historically, even though all the things that we've been through, long term, the markets have always performed. And so, you have to stop being afraid to put your money at risk, and have it working for you."

According to Goldman Sachs, 10-year stock market returns have averaged 9.2% over the past 140 years. But between 2010 and 2020, the S&P 500 has had an average return of 13.6%.

That tells the story. One way to cut into the wealth gap is to get Black folks to invest in stocks.

Compound interest

Albert Einstein called compound interest the eighth wonder of the world. "He who understands it earns it; he who doesn't pays it."

Basically, compound interest is interest on interest. It is the result of reinvesting interest. Here's how it works. You have $1,000 to invest. At 5 percent interest, in one year that $1,000 is worth $1,050. But in the second year you are paid 5 percent interest on your original investment, plus the first year's return of $50 - or $1050. Thus, the return after the second year is $1,102.50. After 10 years, assuming you did not add any money to your principal, your balance is $1,628.89.

Now imagine if you added $100 a month to this account. In one year, you will have $2,250. In two years, you will have $3,562.50 and 10 years you will have a balance of $16,722.39.

Here's a chart that shows what would happen to your same $1,000 in 25 years. You end up with more than $60,000.

Total Savings in US Dollars

Years	Future Value (5.00%)	Total Contributions
Year 0	$1,000.00	$1,000.00
Year 1	$2,250.00	$2,200.00
Year 2	$3,562.50	$3,400.00
Year 3	$4,940.63	$4,600.00
Year 4	$6,387.66	$5,800.00
Year 5	$7,907.04	$7,000.00
Year 6	$9,502.39	$8,200.00
Year 7	$11,177.51	$9,400.00
Year 8	$12,936.39	$10,600.00
Year 9	$14,783.21	$11,800.00
Year 10	$16,722.37	$13,000.00
Year 11	$18,758.48	$14,200.00
Year 12	$20,896.41	$15,400.00
Year 13	$23,141.23	$16,600.00
Year 14	$25,498.29	$17,800.00
Year 15	$27,973.20	$19,000.00
Year 16	$30,571.86	$20,200.00
Year 17	$33,300.46	$21,400.00
Year 18	$36,165.48	$22,600.00
Year 19	$39,173.75	$23,800.00
Year 20	$42,332.44	$25,000.00
Year 21	$45,649.06	$26,200.00
Year 22	$49,131.52	$27,400.00
Year 23	$52,788.09	$28,600.00
Year 24	$56,627.50	$29,800.00
Year 25	$60,658.87	$31,000.00

Rule of 72, or how to double your money in 7 years

It's a simple rule. Figure out your expected annual return and divide it by 72 and you will figure out how long it will take to double your money. Using the same 5 percent return from the compounding example and starting with the same $1,000 investment, we come up with 72/5 or 14.4. It will take more than 14 years to double your money to $2,000. At 9 percent it will take 8 years to double your investment. And if you get lucky and get a 12 percent return, your money will double in six years.

We used $1,000 to simplify the example. But let's go with a larger number, say $10,000. Let's keep the return realistic, say 6 percent. In six years your $10,000 will double to $20,000.

Try plugging in various interest rates from the different accounts your money is in, from savings and money market accounts to index and mutual funds. For example, if your account earns:[29]

1%, it will take **72 years** for your money to double (72 / 1 = 72)
3%, it will take **24 years** for your money to double (72 / 3 = 24)
6%, it will take **12 years** for your money to double (72 / 6 = 12)
9%, it will take **8 years** for your money to double (72 / 9 = 8)
12%, it will take **6 years** for your money to double (72 / 12 = 6)

Risk

There are reasons you should be wary of the market, but that does not mean you should avoid it entirely. We've talked about why you should invest in stocks. But still, there is a chance you will lose some or all of your investment.

There are a few risks involved with the market: economic risk, inflation risk, market risk (including volatility and timing) and the risk of being too conservative.

Black Americans tend to fall into the too conservative category. Understandably, one reason for that is if you have less money, you're less likely to want to risk it.

If you visit a financial planner, one of the first things they will do is assess your risk. They will give you a risk tolerance questionnaire before they do anything else. For example, an investor with a low risk tolerance will favor investments that focus on maintaining your original investment. An aggressive investor will have a high-risk tolerance and is willing to lose money in order to get a better return on his investment. Most people are somewhere in between.

But keep in mind a couple of rules. If you are investing with a long-term horizon, you should be comfortable with a higher-level risk. That's why some financial advisors recommend that if you are in your 20s, 30s or even your 40s, you should be 100 percent invested in stocks. You have plenty of time to recover from the market's down years.

If you are older, or just nervous, you should stick to a more conservative portfolio. The last thing you want to do is freak out every time the Dow goes down a couple of hundred points.

Stocks

You should not start out investing in individual stocks. Even the experts have trouble picking individual stocks. You need to make sure you have a balanced portfolio. In other words, you should not be invested in all retail stocks or all bank stocks. Spread your money among sectors. You'll get much better portfolio balance, and less stress by investing in a mutual fund or an exchange traded fund (ETF).

Mutual Funds

There are big advantages to any investor, especially new investors, to put money into a mutual fund. You can take advantage of the stock market without the worry of which stocks to invest in. The mutual fund manager will decide which invest in. It could be a combination of stocks, bonds and other investments. The mutual fund gives small investors access to a professionally managed portfolio. There are a variety of fees that you may be subject to. The average fee is about 1.40 percent, but some can be much higher.

Exchange Traded Funds (ETFs)

The ETFs offer the same diversification as mutual funds, but at a lower price. They are usually tied to a stock index, like the S&P 500 or the Dow 100.

Pensions and other retirement plans

Most people have most of their wealth in 401(k)s and other workplace retirement accounts. So, it's important to understand what each has to offer.

But roughly half of Americans do not have access to any kind of retirement plan in their workplaces.

Pensions

Our parents and grandparents had pensions. That's not the case today. The number of private companies offering pensions, or defined benefit plans, has gone from 60 percent to less than 14 percent. Chances are if you have a pension today, you are a local, state or federal government employee.

Companies found that it was too expensive to have pensions, so they created the defined contribution plan, or 401(k)-type products. The big difference is all the pressure is now on you, the employee, to figure out how much to contribute and make the investments and make sure it's funded. That hasn't worked well for Black Americans. We have an average of $29,000 saved in our employee sponsored 401(k)s as opposed to $106,000 for the average White American.

More than half of Americans are not covered by any kind of retirement savings plan, whether it's because they are part time or work for a company that does not provide the benefit.

Still, you should understand the different types of accounts.

CHAPTER 06

Traditional 401(k) and "free money"

A 401(k) is an employer-sponsored retirement account. Employees are allowed to deduct a certain percentage of their paycheck for deposit into the 401(k) account, pre-tax. The plan, which is generally managed by a large investment company, like Fidelity or Vanguard, offers you a range of investment options, that are mostly mutual funds, bonds and low-risk savings-type accounts.

Contributions are pre-tax, which means they are deducted before taxes are withheld. The money grows tax-free, but Uncle Sam will get paid. When you begin withdrawals, you must pay ordinary income taxes. If you withdraw your funds early, before 59 ½, you will pay both the tax and a 10 percent early withdrawal penalty. You are required to begin making withdrawals at 72 or you will face tax huge tax penalties of up to 50 percent of the amount you were supposed to withdraw.

Matching contributions are usually made by the employer, either dollar for dollar or 50 cents on the dollar, usually up to 4 or 5 percent. You should at least put in enough so that you can get your employer's "free" matching money.

Financial planner Eric Bailey recalls a client who was making a six-figure income with an employer who matched up to 11% of her retirement contributions, but was only contributing 2% of her salary. "She didn't get it," he said. "She said she never thought about it. She was leaving $27,000 on the table. Assuming it earns six percent, you're talking about $400,000 that's not available in retirement age that she could have had."

For 2021 the maximum contribution from an employee is $19,500. People aged 50 and older can contribute an additional $6,500 in what is called a catch-up.

Roth 401(k)

The rules for contributions are basically the same as they are for a traditional 401(k). The difference is that contributions are made after-tax. So why should you invest in a Roth? Because your money grows tax free in the account, and since you've already paid taxes, there are no taxes to pay when you begin withdrawals. This is important in retirement, when withdrawals are considered ordinary income and can bump you into a higher tax bracket.

403(b) Plan

It is like a 401(k), but the 403(b) plan is a tax-deferred retirement account for employees of public schools, universities and tax-exempt organizations (teachers, school administrators, professors, government employees, nurses, doctors, and librarians, etc.).

457 Plan

Again, like the 401(k), the 457 plans are offered to employees of state and local governments and some nonprofit employers.

Individual Retirement Account (IRA)

The IRA, like the 401(k), is a tax advantaged account. But this account is not connected to the workplace and is established by the individual. Your income and whether you have a plan at work will determine what kind of IRA you qualify for. Contributions are tax deductible, but when you make withdrawals, you pay those taxes. Also, if you make withdrawals before 59 ½, you will pay a 10 percent penalty. Annual contribution limits are $6,000 ($7,000 if you are 60 or older).

Roth Individual Retirement Account

Unlike the Roth 401(k) there are strict income limits on a Roth IRA. But the function is basically the same as a Roth 401(k). Funds go into the account after taxes, and the money in the account grows tax free. Since taxes have been already paid, withdrawals are not taxable. But there is an early withdrawal penalty like all 401(k)s and IRAs.

Required Minimum Distributions

All traditional retirement accounts require you to begin withdrawals after you reach 72. If you fail to make the required withdrawals, you can be penalized up to 50 percent of the amount you were required to withdraw.

529 Plans

A 529 plan is a savings plan that is designed to encourage savings for future tuition costs for your children or grandchildren. Originally intended only for college tuition and costs, they were expanded several years ago to include K-12 educational costs. The plans, which are tax advantaged, can be sponsored by states or educational institutions. There are two types of 529 plans: prepaid tuition plans and education savings plans. They are offered by all 50 states and the District of Columbia. Prepaid tuition plans are offered by many colleges and universities. There are both federal and state tax advantages, assuming you invest in a plan in the state in which you reside.

Education Savings Plans let the saver open an investment account to save specifically for the future higher education expenses of a beneficiary, like a child or a grandchild. Qualified expenses include tuition, mandatory fees and room and board. As with a 401(k), the holder can invest in a variety of mutual funds. Withdrawals can be used to for any college or university, or up to $10,000 per year for tuition at any elementary or secondary school.

Prepaid Tuition plans can only be used at participating colleges and universities for future tuition costs and mandatory fees. They cannot be used for future room and board costs and cannot be used for elementary and secondary schools. The advantage to these plans is they allow you to lock in tuition costs and the participating college or university. And they are usually restricted to the participating college or university.

Civil Service Retirement System (CSRS)

CSRS ended for new employees on when the Federal government, like many big private employers at the time, began to move to less costly defined contribution plans like the 401(k). The government created the Thrift Savings Plan, or TSP. Today only 5 percent of government employees still participate in the CSRS, and most of them are in their late 60s.

Federal Employee Retirement System (FERS)

This retirement plan provides benefits from three different sources: A Basic Benefit Plan, Social Security and the Thrift Savings Plan (TSP). Two of the three parts of FERS, Social Security and the TSP can go with you to your next job if you leave the Federal Government before you retire. When you retire you receive annuity payments each month for life.

Thrift Savings Plan (TSP)

It's a basically defined contribution in which the government matches federal employees' contributions of up to 5 percent of their salary. It operates much like the private sector's 401(k) plan. It offers both the conventional pre-tax plan and a Roth option.

Health Savings Accounts (HSA)

A health savings account lets you set aside money on a pre-tax basis to pay for qualified medical expenses. You can use it to pay for deductibles, copayments, coinsurance, and some other expenses. Because you are paying with pre-tax dollars, which means they reduce your federal and state tax liability. You generally cannot use money from the accounts to pay insurance premiums.

Withdrawals are tax-free. And, unlike a 401(k) or IRA, you are not required to begin withdrawing funds at a certain age. And the money can be carried over from year to year.

You can only contribute to an HSA if you have a high deductible health care plan at work and you cannot open one if you qualify for Medicare. In 2021 the minimum deductible for a high deductible plan to qualify is

$1,400 for an individual and $2,800 for a family. These high-deductible insurance plans (and thus HSAs) are more popular with higher-income individuals who can afford the out-of-pocket expenses.

Annuities

Most of us worry about running out of money in retirement. That's true no matter how much you earn or have saved. And for most of us there's good reason for those concerns. We haven't saved enough for retirement, especially considering that life expectancies make it not only possible, but probable, that we will live into our 90s.

For those who have pensions, it's less of a worry. We know that we'll have a monthly stream of income, some of us for life.

But today only 14 percent of full-time private industry workers have a pension, the Bureau of Labor Statistics estimates. In this new, do-it-yourself world of retirement, most of us save in a company-sponsored 401(k), an IRA, or another plan. Even if we have accumulated a big nest egg, we are left to ourselves to figure out how to turn that money into a stream of income to last a lifetime.

An annuity is one way to do that if you don't have a pension. Many financial planners recommend that you put at least a portion of your retirement savings into an annuity. But because they are not liquid, you should limit the portion of your portfolio invested in them.

And over the years they have gotten a bad reputation, as unscrupulous salesmen have pushed them to people who should not be invested in them just so they can collect the fees and commissions.

I got an email from a retired gentleman when I was writing a column for the Washington Post. One of those unscrupulous insurance salesmen had convinced him and his wife to tie up 90 percent of their assets in annuities. I'm sure he collected hefty commissions on the sales of those annuities. But he had left this couple in a precarious situation. One of the drawbacks to annuities is that the money you invest is no longer liquid, and early liquidation costs can be high. He had already complained to their salesman's boss, to no avail. The only recommendation I could make at that point was to file complaints with state and local authorities.

It's stories like that that make people wary of annuities. But they can be a good thing. First, let's cover the basics.

An annuity is a contract with an insurance company generally purchased for future income in retirement. In return, the owner receives payments at regular intervals. All annuities are not alike. The basic types are:

- **Variable annuity:** This is invested in mutual funds or a pool of managed investments. The advantage is that you benefit if the market rises. The disadvantages are that you pay fees and can lose principal in a down market.
- **Fixed annuity:** This has no fees and will pay you a guaranteed rate of return — for example, 5 percent a year.
- **Fixed-index annuity:** This gives you exposure to the market but at no risk of loss to your principal. It is basically a fixed annuity with a variable rate of return based on an index, such as the Standard & Poor's 500-stock index. The disadvantage: The upside is capped.
- **Immediate annuity:** The investor gives the insurer a lump sum in return for a set rate of return and regular income payments until death, or for a specified period. There are no fees.

The thing an annuity can do well is to provide a hedge against the risk of living far longer than you thought you would. There are instances where an annuity is critical for people's retirement. In cases where someone needs a constant stream of payments for the rest of their lives it would make sense.

But if you need the money to live on, don't risk it. Do not risk what you can't lose. And don't buy an annuity unless you understand how it fits in with your financial plan and your retirement plan. Also make sure you understand the fees. High fees will lower you investment.

And do your homework. First understand the different types of annuities and shop around. You should discuss the investment with your financial advisor to see if an annuity fits in with your portfolio and which type of annuity makes the most sense for you and your family.

Now for the final question. Should annuities be an option for Black Americans. And I've only seen one study address that question. That report says: "Blacks actually benefit more from annuities than Whites, despite having a lower life expectancy, because their lifespans are more uncertain.[30]

Turning your savings into guaranteed lifetime income

We are inundated with advice on how to save and invest. There are millions of articles and thousands of books with all kinds of advice.

But when people get near retirement age and prepare to leave their jobs, they have no idea how to turn those savings into income that will replace their wages. You need to put just enough effort into drawing down your savings as you did in building it up. Otherwise, you will be faced with one of people's biggest fears – running out of money in retirement. There are a variety of strategies, mostly dependent on where and how you save.

Pensions

As a result of companies shifting from pensions to 401(k)s, today only 14 percent of employees at private companies have pensions. Pensions are more prevalent among state, local and government employees. But there are still plenty of Baby Boomers who still have pensions, though many are frozen, meaning companies are no longer contributing to them. But there are four ways to take your pension.

Single life annuity. A single life annuity is the simplest type of pension annuity. Generally, it provides the largest monthly payments of all the pension annuity options. But upon your death the payments stop - even if you die immediately after signing up. That could leave your family without income.

Joint survivor annuity. This option pays you a set amount for as long as you live, and then makes payments to your designated survivor for as long as they live. This option pays less monthly than the single survivor annuity but ensures that your family continues to receive income if you pass away.

Lump sum. You are basically cashing out your pension and moving it away from the company you have worked for. The benefit is that you can move your money to an investment account that offers many more investment options. But you will not receive the monthly annuity payments. You will have to figure out how much to take monthly so as not to deplete your savings.

Period certain option. Some pensions allow participants to take a higher payout and receive the pension for a certain period, such as 10, 15 or 20 years. With this option, even if the pensioner dies, the checks will continue for his or her spouse or heirs for the remainder of the period.

The 4 percent rule

For years financial planners have recommended a rather simple rule for making your money last in retirement. The basic rule is that you withdraw no more than 4 percent of your retirement savings a year, providing a steady stream of income. Theoretically, the income would be generated by interest and dividends while keeping your savings intact. The rule should be considered a rule of thumb, as longevity and many other factors come into play. Basically, it is an attempt to keep people from depleting their savings before they die. But it should not be considered a hard and fast rule.

Annuity

You can achieve the same results of a pension by investing in an annuity. We explained the types of annuities earlier in this chapter.

07

The power (and the danger) of becoming a 401(k) millionaire

CHAPTER 07

Before we get into what it takes to be a 401(k) millionaire, let's briefly look at the average 401(k) balance by age from Vanguard, one of the nation's largest 401(k) plan administrators.

The Average 401k Account Balance by Age[31]

Age	Average 401K Balance	Median 401K Balance
22-25	$4,236	$1,427
25-34	$21,970	$8,126
35-44	$61,238	$22,123
45-54	$115,497	$40,243
55-64	$171,623	$61,739
65+	$192,877	$58,035

Source: Vanguard.com, How America Saves, 2019

Vanguard says the average 401(k) balance is $106,478. But most people don't have anywhere near that much saved for retirement. The median balance is a much better indicator of what we have saved for retirement, and that's $25,775. (The median is that number where half the numbers are lower, and half are higher. The average is the total of those numbers divided by the number of items in that set of numbers.)

Those numbers make it clear that most of us do not save anywhere near enough for retirement. The numbers also make it clear how much hard work and discipline it takes for someone to accumulate $1 million in their plans by the time they reach retirement age.

Fidelity Investments does a quarterly report on the number of customers with $1 million or more in their retirement accounts. Their latest figures put that number at 262,000. (Keep in mind that we're only talking about Fidelity accounts here, but Fidelity is the nation's largest provider of workplace 401(k) plans.)

These are not big-time hedge fund managers or corporate bankers. These are everyday people who did the right things to take advantage of their company-sponsored 401(k) plans.

CHAPTER 07

What are the characteristics of these people? According to Fidelity:

- They save more than 20 percent of their salaries in their 401(k)s and have been saving at high rates throughout their careers.
- They tend to be heavily invested in stocks (as opposed to more conservative bond fund and money market funds). They typically have 75% to 80% of their investments in stocks.
- They don't take out loans on their 401(k)s. Most companies allow employees to take out loans on their fund balance to buy homes or to get them through emergencies. While the loans are free and you pay interest to yourself, you lose the growth on the amount of the loan and many times the employee stops or reduces their contributions while they repay the loan.
- Many said they had some financial planning advice.

Now let's look at how long it might take to grow your 401(k) to a million. There are many 401(k) retirement calculators out there. We'll use the Bankrate calculator.

Let's start out with an employee who earns $50,000 at age 30 and contributes 10 percent of her salary to her retirement account with an employer match of up to 6 percent of her salary. Assuming a 7 percent return over 35 years, she would retire a millionaire.

Current 401(k) balance	$1,000
Years to invest	35
Annual Rate of return	7%
Annual salary	$50,000
Expected annual salary increase	2%
Percent to contribute	10%
Your annual 401(k) contribution	$5,000
Your annual employer match	$1,500
Total you will contribute	$254,971.83
Total your employer will contribute	$76,491.55
Total at age 65	**$1,180,972**

Now let's look at the same 30-year-old earning the same salary but is saving 20 percent of her salary into the company 401(k). She begins with the same $1,000 balance.

Current 401(k) balance	$1,000
Years to invest	35
Annual rate of return	7%
Annual Salary	$50,000
Expected salary increase	2%
Percent to contribute	20%
Your annual contribution	$10,000
Your annual employer match	$1,500
Total you will contribute	$509,943.66
Total your employer will contribute	$76,491.55
Total at age 65	**$2,081,203**

These two examples are meant to show what happens if you exceed your employer match. And those are the characteristics of the people who approach retirement with retirement savings of $1 million or more. Contributing just 5 percent of your salary at the same returns you would end up with $685,000 (with the employer match)

Lots of things can get in the way when we save for retirement – marriage, children, buying homes and cars, school and college tuition – but the 401(k) millionaires found a way to continue saving or somehow make up for the years when they couldn't save as much.

Keep these things in mind

For most people, the 401(k) is the most money they have ever seen in their lives. The biggest danger is that you don't look at it for what it really is – the money that has to keep you in your current lifestyle for the remainder of your life after you retire.

CHAPTER 07

1. It can be easy to overspend

With today's longevity, you might live for another 30 years after you retire. Look at the number of people who are living into their 80s and 90s today. You need to make sure that money will last.

At the same time, keep in mind what generally happens when people come into a lot of money and aren't used to having a lot of money. According to the National Endowment for Financial Education, a whopping 70 percent of the people who win big in a lottery are bankrupt within a few years.

Get the help of a financial planner. And know how much you can spend. For years, the rule was you should not spend more than 4 percent of your retirement savings in any year. Under that rule, if you have saved $1 million, you should not be spending more than $40,000 a year. That is not a hard and fast rule, and, that number does not include Social Security, home value or any other savings and investments you may have accumulated.

Financial planners often tell stories of clients who, when they leave their jobs, see the big check and pay cash for cars or other luxuries. There is nothing wrong with finally living your dream and buying that Recreational Vehicle or taking that dream vacation to Hawaii. But make sure it is budgeted and planned and be sure to discuss it with your financial planner.

2. If you are too conservative, your money will be safe, but it won't grow

You will be fine as long as you keep in mind that the money has to last you for a lifetime. You can make it grow by keeping it invested. The old rule was to keep the percentage of stocks in your portfolio equal to your age. That meant if you were 60, your portfolio would have been 60 percent stocks and 40 percent in less volatile bonds because the older you get, the less risk you should take with your money.

But the rules have changed because people live longer. You want your money to grow, even in retirement. There's a chance you will live into your 90s, and you don't want to run out of money before you die. You may also want to make sure there is an inheritance to leave to your children and grandchildren.

CHAPTER 07

3. Remember, you haven't paid your taxes yet

Here's something that many people forget. Contributions to your 401(k) are tax deferred, not tax-free. You didn't pay federal taxes when the money went into your account, but when you make your withdrawals Uncle Sam will be paid.

Withdrawals from your retirement account will generally be considered ordinary income for tax purposes, based on your tax bracket. If a withdrawal comes directly to you the provider is required to withhold a mandatory 20 percent. That 20 percent may or not cover your tax liabilities. Make sure you consult with a tax professional before your withdrawal.

Take for example the long-time client who retired from a government job and immediately bought a new BMW. She didn't tell her financial advisor because she knew he would recommend against it. She was right. He told her she couldn't afford it (she was not a 401(k) millionaire). Luckily, she was able to return the vehicle within the time allotted. But one thing she had not even considered was the taxes. Her tax bill alone was probably going to be $20,000 after the withdrawal.

Keep in mind that since withdrawals are counted as ordinary income by the IRS, combined with your salary it could bump you into another tax bracket if you do not plan properly.

Finally, if you make a withdrawal before you reach age, 59½ there is a mandatory 10 percent IRS penalty. That combined with the taxes could be a huge hit.

If you are leaving your job, you can roll over your 401(k) into an Individual Retirement Account. That transaction would be tax free. Again, consult a financial professional before you do this. It is always best that the money never comes to you in a check. Roll it over directly from your old 401(k) provider to the new financial institution where you are moving the money in an IRA. Otherwise, the IRS might see the entire account as part of your income for that year.

08

How to decide when you should take Social Security

Black Americans depend heavily on Social Security as they age. Unlike White Americans, they are less likely to have other retirement benefits, such as a pension or a workplace 401(k) plan. Only 44% of Black Americans have retirement savings accounts, with a typical balance of around $20,000, compared to 65% of White Americans, who have an average balance of $50,000, according to the Federal Reserve.

In fact, Social Security is the sole source of income for nearly a third of Black seniors 65 and older) vs. 47 percent of White seniors.

We discussed some of the reasons in the first two chapters of the book. Structural racism and discrimination have forced many Black Americans into lower-wage jobs and even well-educated Black Americans often earn less than their White counterparts. That means they pay less into the Social Security system.

Black Americans are also faced with health inequities and suffer from many long-term health issues such as high blood pressure and diabetes at much higher rates than White Americans. Black Americans suffer disproportionally from eight of the top 13 top causes of death in the U.S. – heart disease, stroke, cancer, influenza and pneumonia, diabetes, HIV disease, kidney failure and homicide, says Dr. Ebony Jade Hilton, associate professor of Anesthesiology and Critical Care Medicine at University of Virginia and an outspoken critic of racial health inequities.

What does all that have to do with Social Security?

The fact is: Black Americans are in a vicious cycle of poverty and dependence on Social Security. They take it early – often before full retirement age - because they must. They are in lower paying jobs that they physically can't perform as they age. They have to leave because of their own health issues or to become caretaker for a family member. Black women, in particular, are forced to leave the job force for years at a time because they have to provide childcare for their children or grandchildren. They are thus paying less into the system and receiving less in benefits.

One of the biggest problems in taking Social Security early is that you are literally leaving hundreds of thousands of dollars on the table.

To understand how to stop this vicious cycle, we need a better understanding of Social Security laws, why taking it early means reduced benefits for life and why waiting for a year or two can make a big difference in your monthly check.

Keep this in mind. Social Security was never meant to be a sole source of retirement income for anyone. It was always meant to supplement your retirement savings and pension.

The average Social Security check is only about $1,500. And yet, 30 percent of Black seniors depend on it as their sole source of income.

What is full retirement age?

Full retirement age is the age when you are entitled to receive 100 percent of your Social Security benefits. The amount is based on your lifetime of earnings. If you were born between 1943 and 1954, your full retirement age is 66. If you were born in 1955, it is 66 and 2 months. For those born between 1956 and 1959, it increases gradually. If you were born in 1960 or later, your full retirement age is 67.

Benefits are based on 35 years of earnings. Then, the 10 years of your highest earnings are used for the final computations.

Most beneficiaries claim benefits before the full retirement age. In 2019, when the full retirement was 66 and six months, 33 percent of new beneficiaries were 62; 60 percent were under the age of 66.[32]

Workers who take their Social Security early, or when they are first eligible, receive benefits that are 30 percent less than they would have been had they waited. Workers who delay benefits after full retirement age can see an increase in benefits of about 8 percent for each year that they wait. Waiting even one year can make a difference. What you receive will be unchanged (except for cost-of-living increases) for the remainder of your life.

Of course, the amount of your benefits depends on many factors, as discussed above, but waiting until 70 can increase your benefits from the $1,500 you might receive at 62 to $3,000 at 70. You can go to SSA.gov to determine how much you will receive at 62 and how much you will receive if you wait.

Whether or not you should wait depends on many factors, including your health, your family's health history and whether you can financially afford to wait. A financial planner can help you figure out the most opportune time to file. Many now make Social Security an integral part of their financial plans. If you don't think you can afford a financial planner, all is not lost. Many Black financial planners do pro bono work and give back to the community by giving free seminars and courses at schools and community centers.

When you should consider waiting

Longevity is probably the biggest issue to consider. When Social Security was started during the Depression in 1935 the retirement age was 65, but life expectancy at birth was 58 for men and 62 for women.

Today, because older people are generally more fit and because of the huge advances in health care and medicine, people live longer.

In 2020, life expectancy at birth for the total U.S. population was 77.8 years, according to the Centers for Disease Control. Life expectancy at birth for males was 75; for women, 80.5 years.

But here are some startling numbers. According to the Society of Actuaries, a 65-year-old male today in average health has a 35 percent chance of living to 90 while the odds for a woman in similar health is 46 percent. For a 65-year-old couple today there is a 50 percent chance that both will live past 80 and that one will live another 27 years.

The point is that's a lot of years to live on minimum Social Security benefits with 1 percent annual cost-of-living increases.

CHAPTER 08

Why it may not make sense to wait

You need the money. We've already talked about some of the economic challenges facing some Black Americans. We know many take Social Security because they have no other source of income.[33]

- 45 percent of Blacks rely on Social Security for 90 percent or more of their income compared to 29 percent of Whites.
- 33 percent of Blacks rely on Social Security for *all* their income compared with only 16 percent of Whites.

There are few alternatives if you have no other sources of income, and you are unable to work.

Calculating your break-even age. Ken Moriaf, a Certified Financial Planner, author and radio show host, did the math in a Kiplinger article.

The timing of your Social Security benefits is important — it could make a difference of thousands of dollars in your retirement income. And though there are many factors to consider when deciding about Social Security, it's simple to calculate your Social Security break-even age. Let's use an example to illustrate the calculation:

Jeff has reached full retirement age and is deciding whether to begin collecting benefits now or to delay for one year. If he collects now, he'll receive $1,000 per month. But like everyone else, if he waits to take his benefit, it will increase by 8% each year after his full retirement age. In other words, if Jeff waits a year to apply for benefits, he'll get $80 more, for a total of $1,080 per month. If Jeff decided to wait that year, how long would it take him to break even?

Essentially Jeff forfeited $12,000 ($1,000 times 12) but gained $80 a month. To find out his break-even age, Jeff would divide $12,000 by $80 a month, which comes out to 150 months or 12 ½ years. So, if Jeff waits for one year, it will take him 12 ½ years to get back to even. Therefore, if Jeff thinks he'll live more than 12 ½ years, it could make sense to delay taking Social Security because he would eventually come out ahead. If not, he may want to take his benefits now.[34]

CHAPTER 08

Black Americans have a shorter life expectancy

Due to economic and health disparities, "Black Americans live shorter and sicker lives than their White counterparts, said Tyson Brown, associate professor of sociology at Duke University.

"Many Black older Americans have endured decades of overt and subtle forms of discrimination in educational, criminal justice systems, and healthcare systems as well as in jobs, housing, credit and consumer markets," he said.

They also have the lowest levels of income and wealth, which often means they often need to continue working. Yet, their health problems limit their ability to continue working, he said. "And so, it's sort of a Catch-22, that they're often sort of put in a bind there."

According to the CDC, from 2019 to the first half of 2020, life expectancy decreased 2.7 years for Black Americans, from 74.7 to 72, because of the Covid epidemic. It dropped 0.8 years for White Americans, to 78. Life expectancy for Black men dropped three years while life expectancy for Black women dropped 2.4 years, the CDC said.

Of course, we have no idea how long we will live. But when deciding on when to take Social Security you must consider your health as well as your family's health history. If there is a history of heart problems or cancer in your family history, you may want to take Social Security sooner rather than later.

My Social Security

To see where you stand in terms of Social Security you should go to www.ssa.gov and create a "my Social Security" account. You can check your earnings history for accuracy and see what your benefits will be at what age. That's important that you do that online since the Social Security Administration has moved away from paper statements in recent years.

09

How credit scores help worsen the racial wealth gap

Economists and credit experts have reached the same conclusions that Black Americans have known for years: Credit scores are considerably worse for Black Americans than for White Americans and add significantly to the racial wealth gap.

More than 50% of White households had a FICO credit score above 700, compared with only 21% of Black households, according to a 2017 study by the Urban Institute[35], a Washington, D.C. think tank. A credit score of 700 or higher is often required for borrowers to be eligible for the best interest rates on many types of loans, including mortgage loans and car loans.

Lisa D. Cook, economist at Michigan State University and a former senior economist at the White House Council of Economic Advisers under the Obama administration, said credit scores help worsen the wealth gap. Besides determining eligibility for loans, they are also considered by landlords for apartment rentals and even companies reviewing job candidates.

"Discrimination has harmed Black Americans' creditworthiness," Cook said. "Statistically, Black Americans are at a financial disadvantage: They earn less, they are saddled with higher-interest debt, and they are less likely to own a home than White Americans. "We need to reverse the damage.[36]"

A survey from Credit Sesame, a credit and loan company came to the same conclusion: Blacks are being hit hard by the credit system. "Poor credit impacts more than just one's financial picture—it can affect everything from a consumer's mental health to their ability to get a car loan or lease a cell phone—this racial credit gap comes at a high cost," the company said in releasing its survey. Among the findings in the report:

- 54 percent of Black Americans report having poor or fair credit (a credit score below 640) or no credit at all vs. 37 percent of White Americans.
- More than half (53 percent) of Black Americans say they are living paycheck to paycheck, significantly higher than 44 percent of Americans overall.

- 21 percent of Black Americans say they have student loans compared to 13 percent of all Americans. Fifty-three percent of Black Americans said they have a credit card—a critical component for building a strong credit foundation — compared to 67 percent of White Americans.

"We live in a credit driven society. So, it's important that you manage credit well because it gives you the opportunity to leverage your income, and you get credit to acquire the things that you need," said Theodore Daniels, founder and CEO of the non-profit Society for Financial Education and Professional Development (SFE&PD). "Credit plays a very key role in your life. You must understand how to use it because if you have credit, you have a big pot of money waiting for you that is greater than your savings account."

But it's critically important that you make payments on time because late or slow payments will increase your risk to lenders in the future.

What is a credit score?

Let's start with the basics. A credit score is a three-digit number on a scale of 300 to 850, that companies use to estimate how likely you are to repay money or pay your bills. Where your score falls in this range represents your "credit risk."

Your credit scores can affect whether a lender approves you for a mortgage, auto loan, personal loan, credit card or other type of credit. If you're approved for a loan, it can also help determine the interest rate you're offered.

A low credit score could also mean that you pay more for car insurance or that utilities may require a deposit before approving you for service. Many apartment owners and landlords also use your credit score to determine if they want you as a tenant.

Credit scores are calculated using the information in your credit reports. Each of the three main consumer credit bureaus — Equifax, Experian and TransUnion — produces a credit report with information from lenders, credit card issuers and other financial institutions.

CHAPTER 09

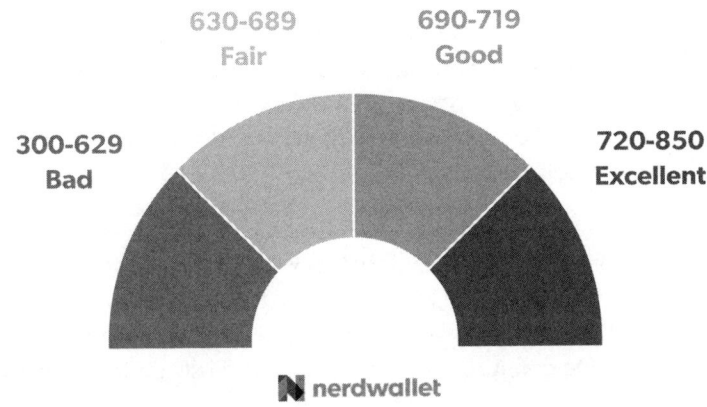

Your credit reports include information about your credit history and activity. Scores are typically based on factors such as your history of paying bills, the amount of your available credit you're using and the types of debt you have.

Here's how your score is calculated according to myFICO.com: 35 percent is based on your payment history; 30 percent is based on your outstanding debt; 15 percent, the length of your credit history; 10 percent new credit; and 10 percent your credit mix (your mix of credit cards, installment credit, finance company loans, retail credit and mortgage loans.)

Student loans

Americans owed more than $1.7 trillion in student loan debt in 2021. The average student loan debt was nearly $38,000.

Student loans have emerged as a big problem for Black Americans. Some parents are paying for the loans of the children while they still have outstanding loans themselves.

Default rates for Black American borrowers remain higher than those for their peers, regardless of the type of higher education institution they attended, according to the Center for American Progress. "Within six years of starting college, one-third of all Black or African American borrowers who had entered repayment defaulted on their loans, compared to just 13 percent of their White peers.[37]" The highest default rates are among students who attended for-profit institutions and students who did not graduate, the report said.

According to one report, Black college graduates owe an average of $25,000 more in student loan debt that White college graduates. And four years after graduation, 48 percent of Black students still owe an average of 12.5% more than they borrowed. They are also more likely than their White counterparts to struggle financially under the load of student debt.[38]

Auto loans

"We (Black Americans) can't move towards creating wealth because we get bogged down and hold loans longer than we should, because we are more payment sensitive," said Daniels. "We like low payments. You may like a $250 (monthly) car loan, but it takes you seven years to pay it off." That's why car salesmen focus on the monthly payment instead of the cost of the car.

Here's a chart from ValuePenguin, a Lending Tree® affiliate that specializes in consumer research. The chart shows how much your credit score can impact the interest charged for a new car loan.

Average Rates by FICO Score: 60 Month Loans on New Cars

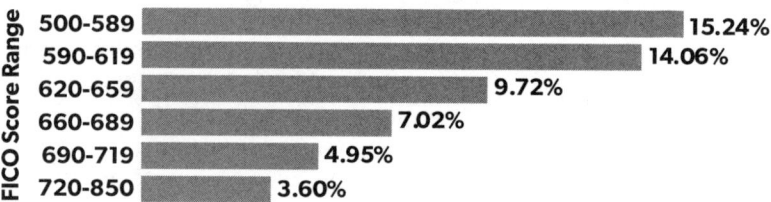

Source: ValuePenguin

In the chart below, let's compare how much people with the worst credit will pay for a car over 5, 6 and 7 years vs. the people with the best credit ratings.

The average cost of a new car in 2020 was nearly $38,000. Let's estimate a 10 percent down payment, or $3,800, so the amount financed will be $34,200. To keep it simple, no trade-in or incentives have been included.

Loan Term	Monthly Payment	Interest Rate	Total Interest
48 months/4 years	$955.98	15.24%	$11,866.92
	$766.10	3.60%	$2,572.66
60 months/5 years	$817.93	15.24%	$14,875.83
	$623.69	3.60%	$3,221.43
72 months/6 years	$727.62	15.24%	$18,188.95
	$528.85	3.60%	$3,877.54
84 months/7 years	$664.56	15.24%	$21,623.25
	$461.20	3.60%	$4,551.00

Payday lenders

Daniels says he counsels clients to not only be payment sensitive but be cost sensitive. "If you have a good credit history and pay your loans on time, you're going to get a lower interest rate. Bad credit can force you to some unattractive alternatives, such as payday lenders, rental centers and pawn shops.

"They are not regulated by the federal government, and the interest rate can be 300%, 400% or 500%. It makes it almost impossible to pay," Daniels said. "Plus, it's a tremendous drainage on households in the African American community."

One report said $139 billion in interest and fees was paid in one year to these alternative financial institutions like payday loans.

Fixing bad credit

1. **Get a copy of your credit report.** Credit Karma, Credit Sesame and several other websites offer free credit scores from the three main credit bureaus: Experian, Equifax and TransUnion. You can get information at www.annualcreditreport.com. While you are entitled to receive a free copy of your credit report from major credit agencies annually, that does not include your credit scores. You can also get your scores from your credit card company or lender, or from a credit counselor.

   If there are inaccuracies, dispute them immediately. Credit agencies must respond to disputes in 30 days and remove incorrect information immediately.

2. **Begin to build a good credit history.** We've already discussed how 35 percent of your credit score is based on your payment history. One late payment can knock you score down a grade and could stay on your credit report for up to seven years. Pay your bills on time. If you can't pay all your bills on time in a particular month, be strategic. Mortgage companies and banks are certain to report a late payment to the credit bureau. Public utilities and mobile phone companies are less likely.

3. **Look at your debt to credit ratio.** If you have $10,000 limit on a credit card and you have used most or all of it, that's a bad sign to lenders. Experts say it's best to keep your usage at 10 to 30 percent of your available credit. One way to improve your ratio is to pay down your balances. This can have an immediate impact on your credit score. You can also achieve this goal by increasing your credit limit.

4. **Pay down total debt.** Make paying off high interest-loans and credit cards the first priority. Even if you can't make a dent in your total debt immediately, you should make it a part of your long-term financial plan. It will make a difference.

10

An estate plan is an essential part of any financial plan

CHAPTER 10

It's still a shock when we hear the stories of the Black celebrities who died without a will: Prince, Aretha Franklin, John Singleton, Bob Marley, former NFL quarterback Steve McNair… Their estates, some worth hundreds of millions of dollars, remain tied up in appeals and litigation years after their deaths. If and when these estates are finally resolved, there's no telling how much will be left for the heirs after lawyers' fees and court costs.

But forget about celebrities for a moment. If you die without a will, your estate could be in probate for a year and the amount of your inheritance reduced five to 10 percent or more, depending on your state. Seven states, including California, allow estate attorneys to charge a percentage of the estate. (Arkansas, Florida, Iowa, Missouri, Montana, and Wyoming are the others.)

According to the AARP 60 percent of Americans do not have a will. Black Enterprise magazine estimates that the number is 70 percent for Black Americans. And what do we lose? We lose the ability to transfer generational wealth, which contributes greatly to the racial wealth gap.

An estate plan is also critical for Black Americans to narrow the wealth gap and pass generational wealth to their children and grandchildren.

Here's another sobering set of numbers. White families are twice as likely to receive an inheritance as Black families, and that inheritance is three times as large.

"For families with an inheritance, median White wealth is 7.5 percent times larger than for Black families. Compatibly, White families have 5.4 times more wealth than Black families without an inheritance. The importance of inheritances to the wealth position of White families is staggering. At the median, in inheritance increases wealth by more than $100,000 for White families and only $4,000 for Black families.[39]

A will is only a part of an estate plan. We'll get into more specifics later in this chapter. But first, let's get an understanding of exactly what is an estate plan. An estate plan is when you "officially put into writing what you want to happen to your assets after you die. You can do this using wills, trusts, advance directives and by designating your beneficiaries on your investment and retirement accounts. Life insurance policies may also be a part of your estate plan.

CHAPTER 10

Dying without a will

Why do so many people put it off? It's a downright scary proposition. Sometimes even thinking about your final wishes can be emotionally draining. They also feel intimidated by the complexities of estate planning and forced to make difficult decisions before they are ready. It's a decision that many put off because it involves dealing with something that they don't want to think about – their own mortality.

But dying without a legal will, which is legally called dying intestate, means that someone other than you or your loved ones will be making the decisions about how your estate will be distributed. It may not be how you intended your assets to be distributed and they may go to people you didn't intend.

Your assets will be distributed through probate courts. The courts will begin that process by appointing an administrator to oversee your estate. Probate laws differ from state to state, but it will be the job of the administrator to locate legal heirs and the court will decide how the assets are distributed.

Getting started. Find an Estate Attorney

The first step in the process should be finding an estate attorney. Ask your trusted friends, colleagues, family members. Also ask people in your sorority and fraternity and religious organizations. Word-of-mouth is one of the best references.

The cost will depend on where you live, the complexity of the estate plan and the lawyer. For example, the cost might be lower for a young couple with young children who are financially secure, but not wealthy. An older couple who are wealthy and one or both were previously married and had children in those previous marriages will be quite a bit more complicated.

Go in with a list of questions. At the top of the list should be their fees.

Some estate attorneys will charge a flat fee for a will or estate plan. Others will charge by the hour. The cost for a more complicated estate plan could cost $250 to $350. A simple will might cost less than a $500 flat fee. But it is more likely to cost $1,000 to $1,200.[40]

Once you have the fees out of the way, meet your top candidates in person. You will be sharing intimate details of your life; you will need to feel comfortable with them. For example, a woman might feel more comfortable with a female estate attorney.

Ask questions about where they went to school, how long have they practiced, how and when will they contact you. Trust your instincts.

Let's be clear. This is not something you should try to do yourself despite the many sites online that offer discount documents that help you create your own will. Here's the problem with that: Every state has a specific set of estate laws. On top of that, every one of us has a unique situation. A high divorce rate has led to a record number of second and third marriages – and blended families. With blended families come more complicated wills and estate plans.

Also, as noted above, estate planning laws and taxes are different in each state. There are 17 states plus the District of Columbia that tax your estate, inheritance, or both, according to the Tax Foundation. Eleven states plus Washington, D.C. have only an estate tax: Connecticut, Hawaii, Illinois, Maine, Massachusetts, Minnesota, New York, Oregon, Rhode Island, Vermont, and Washington. Iowa, Kentucky, Nebraska, New Jersey and Pennsylvania have only an inheritance tax. Maryland taxes both inheritances and estates, the only state to do so.

The estate lawyer is only one member of your financial team. You may need to take a more holistic look at your estate plan. You should consider estate planning, tax planning and financial planning together because they are all interrelated. If you only look at one of these areas at a time, you may create complications in another area and unintentionally increase your expenses or taxes. That means your financial planner, accountant and estate attorney should be a team working together for your benefit. An in-person meeting may be difficult, but you should have your team on a conference call at least once a year.

CHAPTER 10

Next, take an inventory of your assets

Next, take inventory of your assets. It can be extremely frustrating if a spouse, already under a great deal of emotional stress, has to track down paperwork and account information that's scattered around the house, especially if there are multiple accounts at multiple financial institutions.

Get a notebook and list all of your assets. Include home, autos, investment accounts, retirement accounts including 401(k) and pensions. Write down financial institution, approximate balance and account numbers. Also write down all credit card information, account numbers and bank issuer.

Don't forget your personal assets, things you would like to pass to your children or grandchildren. You might include watches, jewelry, china and even furniture.

When it comes time to sit down with an estate lawyer you will most likely not forget to include assets.

What is becoming increasingly important in today's digital world is digital account information and password information. The internet is filled with stories of difficulties surviving spouses have had retrieving passwords of their deceased loved ones. A few years ago, a widow sued Apple because the company wanted a court order before it would share her husband's password. She won her case, but the issue remains a problem.

Many online accounts will not pass through your will or other estate planning devices because technical, they are not your property. Social network accounts, domain name registrations, email accounts and most of the other types of online accounts are licensed. The contract ends upon your death.

However, your executor will need access (i.e., passwords) to these accounts, including savings and investments, pensions and other retirement accounts, utilities and cable, tax preparer, mortgage and life insurance, if for no other reason, to pay bills during the probate process. You should put the passwords in a sealed envelope and make sure your spouse or partner knows where it is. Other options are to give it to your attorney or lock it in a safe, a locked fireproof filing cabinet or a safety deposit box.

Why everyone needs an estate plan:

1. Avoid a drawn-out probate process

Even if you die with a will, your estate will go through probate to implement the provisions of the will. But if you die without a will, the process becomes more complicated. The estate must be distributed based on the state's laws of inheritance. The probate process differs from state to state, but in most states takes a minimum of seven months to allow creditors to put through claims. In addition, it is a public process, allowing anyone and everyone to know your business and everyone to put in a claim.

The probate process can also be expensive, and legal costs will reduce the amount your loved ones inherit.

2. You chose how to distribute your assets

An estate plan allows you to allocate your assets according to your wishes. If you don't have an estate plan, your money and property may not get to the correct person.

Additionally, some people who get an inheritance in one big sum might blow through it quickly. An estate plan can be used to customize inheritances to set restrictions on certain beneficiaries, especially if they are young, immature or irresponsible.

If there is not a will when you die, it is called dying intestate. Each individual state has its own succession formula for who receives money and property left by the deceased. That state would be last in that line of succession if the state can't find a relative.

3. You can minimize taxes

Planning can save your heirs from a big tax bill. For example, your beneficiaries will need to pay income tax on money they inherit in a traditional IRA. However, money you leave them in a Roth IRA can be withdrawn tax-free. An estate plan can create less of a tax burden for your relatives. You heirs can literally be clobbered by taxes if you don't have a trust in place.

4. You can set up care for dependent children

Families with dependent children should plan for childcare if both parents pass away. Many young couples don't think about it, but in the event of both of their untimely deaths, they need to appoint someone to be the guardian of their children.

Make sure that if you have minor children, that you have named someone to be the proper caretaker. That is one of the biggest disputes with small children less than 18. Many don't do an estate plan because they are so uncomfortable having the conversation on who will be the caretaker – my relatives or your relatives.

Understand the difference between a trust vs. a will

A will and a trust both outline who will receive your assets. They just do so in different ways, and each has advantages and disadvantages.

A will allows you to name a guardian for children or pets, designate who receives your assets and specify your funeral arrangements. But your control over the distribution of your assets is limited and your assets will go through probate when you pass away.

A trust offers you more control over when and how your assets are distributed. A will is more likely to be challenged than a trust. Trusts rarely are challenged, partly because their details aren't public. Also, the rules for challenging wills are well-established, while there is less law concerning challenges to trusts.

The trust is named the legal owner of property. Deeds to real estate, titles to vehicles and some other assets have to be reissued in the name of the trust. Vehicle titles and some other assets may also have to be reissued and names on financial accounts might need to be changed.

Your estate attorney can tell you how best to use a will and a trust in your estate plan.

Beneficiary designation

It doesn't matter how old you are or how young you are, you need to update your beneficiary designations every year. There are so many horror stories about people who didn't take the time to update those beneficiaries on financial accounts and their assets going to former spouses and not to the new spouses and the children that were the intended beneficiaries.

One financial planner tells a story of a well-to-do man who never changed his beneficiary on his life insurance to his wife when he got married. When he died, the money went to his mother, who did not care for his wife and would not give her even a portion of the money, even though the mother didn't need it. The widow had no legal recourse.

The person you designate and the beneficiary on 401(k)s, 403(b)s, IRAS, pensions and savings and investment accounts are the final word. Beneficiary designation even trumps a will.

So, it doesn't matter what your intentions are, or even what your will said, the assets will go to the person or persons named as beneficiary.

Planning for children with special needs

Any kind of estate planning can be overwhelming, but you especially need a written plan for a family member who has a disability.

- Your disabled family member might qualify for local or federal benefits, and you might be able to save for their needs in a tax-advantaged ABLE account.
- You might want to consider a trust for an individual with special needs.

The Special Needs Alliance, a national organization of attorneys who practice disability and public benefits law, suggests a meeting with a special needs attorney who is familiar with the unique challenges that a caring for a disabled child brings to the estate planning process, to draft the necessary documents to express how you want your property, finances, health care, and care of your children handled following your death or if you are incapacitated.

Your attorney can also help you set up your financial strategies, such as trusts, to ensure that your child with a disability can continue to maintain a quality life when you are gone. The organization says you should make sure your special needs attorney is familiar with Medicare, Medicaid, Social Security, and Supplemental Security Income.

You might want to plan for pet care after your death

Pets will need to be cared for if the owner passes away. You may want to say who gets custody of pets in death and leave money in a pet trust to make sure animals are taken care of.

Health care directives

Many people just don't realize how critical health care directives and power of attorney can be. A will or trust specifies who will receive your assets when you pass away. But what happens if you become incapacitated, temporarily or permanently.

One veteran financial planner has more than once had a grieving and stressed wife call because her partner was in the hospital and incapacitated or in a coma. They needed access to the money in the husband's account to pay the hospital bill and other expenses. But sadly, the financial planner couldn't do as much as give them an account balance. Why? Because they did not have a power of attorney, even though they were legally married.

By planning in advance, you can not only get the medical care you desire if you are incapacitated, but you will also relieve your loved ones of making major medical decisions during moments of grief or crisis. The family of one of my terminally ill relatives disagreed with every medical decision his spouse made, even though she was following his wishes. But she had his medical power of attorney, so her decisions were final.

The living will, also called an advance healthcare directive, is used when you are incapacitated, mentally incompetent or unable to communicate. It is used only if a person is terminally ill or permanently unconscious. It describes the type of medical treatment you would want to receive or under what conditions doctors should attempt to prolong your life.

Durable power of attorney is a legal document that helps you plan for medical emergencies and declines in mental functioning and can ensure that your finances are taken care of. Having these documents in place helps eliminate confusion and uncertainty when family members must make tough medical decisions. It can also keep your spouse from having to go before a judge to make financial decisions.

Do not resuscitate (DNR) orders. A Do Not Resuscitate or DNR order means that if you stop breathing or your heart stops, nothing will be done to try to keep you alive.

Organ and tissue donation can be included in your advance directive. Many states also provide organ donor cards or add notations to your driver's license.

Admittedly, this can be scary stuff for Black folks. It's a lot to think about, and a lot to do. But think about the alternative. Remember the close friends or family member who passed away without a will and without insurance. And think about the scene: four or five family members sitting around the dining room table, each pitching in their $2,000 to help pay the funeral expenses. And then, think about this: Is this the way you want to be remembered when you pass away?

11

Understanding insurance – and the role it played in creating the racial wealth gap

CHAPTER 11

African Americans have a long and complicated history with the insurance industry. They faced the same racism and discrimination that they faced from virtually every institution in America, financial or otherwise. That's how some of the nation's first Black millionaires made their money. They founded insurance companies that catered to Blacks. In fact, many still exist. The Durham-based North Carolina Mutual Insurance Company, the nation's largest Black insurance company, was founded in 1899.

The Black-owned insurance companies thrived because of the racism and discrimination from White insurance companies, who refused to insure Black Americans, and those that did charged higher rates.

Originally, the White insurance companies charged higher rates for Blacks because the former slaves had higher mortality rates. But these separate rates for Blacks and Whites stretched into the 1960s adding one more piece of historical racism as a major contributor to the racial wealth divide.

Blacks see life insurance as a way to pass generational wealth to their families. A Haven Life survey[41] says that 22 percent of Blacks value life insurance to pass along generational wealth, compared to just 8 percent of White respondents. "This opinion is likely formed from decades of discrimination," the survey says. But that same survey also says the median value of life insurance policies held by Black Americans is $50,000 compared to a median coverage amount of $150,000 among Whites.

Nick Abrams, a CFP® and founder of AJW Financial Partners in Baltimore, Maryland, says Black Americans need to reconsider how they think about life insurance and stop buying the policy that only covers your burial expenses.

"We need to start looking at life insurance as a tool to create wealth for future generations," he said. "Where else can you pay a couple dollars per month and you can leave a six or seven figure, tax-free inheritance to somebody. That's huge. And that's something that we have got to truly start looking at as a way of leaving wealth."

The injustice doesn't stop with life insurance. For decades, auto insurers have charged higher average premiums to drivers living in predominantly minority urban neighborhoods than to drivers with similar safety records living in majority White neighborhoods. Insurers have long defended their pricing by saying that the risk of accidents is greater in those neighborhoods, even for motorists who have never had one.

However, ProPublica and Consumer Reports examined auto insurance premiums and payouts in California, Illinois, Texas, and Missouri, and found that many of the disparities in auto insurance prices between minority and White neighborhoods are wider than can be explained by risk. In some cases, insurers were charging premiums that were on average 30 percent higher in zip codes where most residents are minorities than they were charging in White neighborhoods with similar accident costs.[42]

Also, when it comes to health insurance, African Americans of all ages have lower rates of coverage. Prior to the Affordable care act, 20 percent of Black Americans were uninsured compared to just 13 percent of White Americans.

Of course, this history, like much of what we have discussed, boils down to racism and discrimination and the lack of financial literacy. To that end, we'll now spend some time on an explainer on insurance.

We'll start with whole life vs. term life. Like most other financial planners, I believe the biggest problems with the whole life policies is they try to do two different things - insurance and investing - and in the process makes both more complicated than they need to be.

Life Insurance

Whole life. A few years ago, I was doing a web chat for a newspaper I was writing for at the time and got into a disagreement with a woman about whole life policies. She had held onto one long enough to get a $10,000 payout. My argument was that if she had bought a term life insurance policy and invested in the stock market instead, she would have come out much better. She adamantly disagreed. From 2011 through 2020, the average stock market return was 13.9% annually for the S&P 500 Index. Her return was most likely in the low single digits.

Basically, whole life insurance provides coverage for life. But it also includes an investment component, which is the policy's cash value. That cash value grows slowly in a tax-deferred account from which you can borrow money. If you don't repay that loan, with interest, you will reduce your death benefit. The advantages are that the premium remains the same for life and the death benefit is guaranteed. Also, the cash value grows at a guaranteed rate. Some whole life policies can also earn annual dividends, though they are not guaranteed.

Bankrate.com says whole life is worth it to "some people," such as high-income individuals who have maxed out their tax-deferred investment accounts, like IRAs and 401(k)s or for those who have dependents like children with special needs.

"However, whole life insurance policies are typically expensive. Unless you're getting an amazing Internal Rate of Return (IRR), it's not worth the high premiums. For most people, a term life insurance policy is a better option. The premiums are cheaper, and you can get a similar amount of coverage. It's important to remember that just because whole life insurance has an investment component, doesn't mean it's a great investment strategy. The Internal Rate of Return (anticipated annual growth rate) on a whole life insurance policy is typically very low compared to other investments because life insurance has additional expenses that other investments don't require.[43]"

Term life. Term life insurance is much cheaper because it's temporary and has no cash value; A life insurance policy mainly functions as an income replacement for your family in the event of your death. Term life guarantees this financial protection over a specific term, and then it expires. Terms usually last from 10 to 30 years. You pay a monthly or annual premium, which is determined by your health and demographic information.

Universal life insurance, like whole life, is a permanent insurance, meaning it provides coverage for your entire life. But it offers more flexibility. Most policies allow you to skip premium payments if the cash value is enough to cover your required expenses for that month. Some policies may allow you to increase or decrease the death benefit. You may be able to borrow against the policy. Earned interest accumulates tax deferred.

CHAPTER 11

Variable life insurance gives you direct investment in the stock market. The policies have higher upside potential of earning cash than other permanent life insurance policies. You get to decide how to invest the cash value. But they often come with higher fees than other cash value life insurance policies.

Indexed universal life insurance pays interest based on the movement of stock indexes. These are complex products and not for everyone. Besides a death benefit, you can decide how to invest the cash value. It can be tied to a stock market index, such as the S&P 500. Besides being complex and volatile, they are more expensive than other permanent insurance products.

There are many other options for insurance, including policies that combine life insurance with long-term care insurance. The best advice is to keep it simple, so you understand the pluses and minuses. And if you want to invest in one of the more complicated products, talk to you CFP® or a Certified Public Accountant (CPA) for advice.

Health Insurance

Most Americans get their health insurance through their workplace. According to the Kaiser Family Foundation, 49 percent of Americans get insurance through their jobs. Employers in 2020 paid 67 percent of the costs, or an average of $13,717 according to the U.S. Bureau of Labor Statistics. Annual employee contributions averaged $6,797.

So why are so many workers, especially so many Black workers, uninsured. A report by the Urban Institute says that nearly half of uninsured workers work for firms that don't provide health insurance.

Workers in small firms, and those who work in retail, construction, and service firms, are disproportionately likely to be uninsured. Workers who earn low wages, work part-time, have short job tenure, and who live in households with low incomes are also among the most likely to be uninsured.[44]

Under the Affordable Care Act, or Obamacare, the number of people who were uninsured was reduced by 20 million people.

CHAPTER 11

But the lack of health insurance is not just a low-income problem. There are people who delay retiring or make decisions on whether to take a job based on health insurance. Here we need to address how expensive and difficult it may be for some professionals to obtain health insurance on the open market.

In 2020, the average national cost for health insurance was $456 for an individual and $1,152 for a family per month, according to ehealthinsurance.com. But that number can vary greatly by your location and your health.

I have many friends and colleagues who found out how expensive health care can be the hard way. Some quit their jobs to start businesses. About 94 percent of Black owned businesses are sole proprietorships or partnerships with no paid employees. Many of these small businesses owners have a difficult time getting health insurance for themselves, let alone their employees.

Other colleagues took buyout offers from their jobs and retired early, forgetting that they don't become eligible for Medicare until they turn 65. Others lost their jobs in the COVID-19 pandemic. The effect is the same. They have to find insurance on the open market.

If you retire at 62, whether it is planned or involuntary, you must go on the open market to buy insurance. According to Fidelity, a 65-year-old couple retiring in 2020 can expect to spend $295,000 in health care and medical expenses throughout retirement

This goes back to our earlier chapter on budgeting. Before you initiate any life-changing even, you need to do a budget so you can be aware of the costs.

There are also different types of health insurance.

Generally, you will choose from health plans with different levels of benefits: bronze, silver, gold and platinum. Bronze plans have the least coverage, and platinum plans have the most. The details, however, can vary across plans. In addition, deductibles -- the amount you pay before your plan picks up 100% of your health care costs - vary according to the plan you choose, generally with the least expensive carrying the highest deductible.

Platinum generally covers 90% of your medical costs.

Gold covers 80% on average of your medical costs.

Silver covers 70% on average of your medical costs.

Bronze covers 60% on average of your medical costs.

Now that we understand the levels, let's look at the different types of insurance plans.

HMOs offer a local network of participating doctors, hospitals, and other health care professionals and facilities that you must select from. They also require you to choose a primary care provider (PCP) from the network

EPOs offer a network of participating providers that you must select from. Most EPO plans do not include coverage for out-of-network care except in the case of an emergency.

POS or Point-of-Service Plans, combine features of HMO and PPO plans. The network is generally smaller than a PPO plan, but the costs for in-network care are typically lower. You are required to choose a primary care provider from within your plan's network.

PPOs generally offer a large network of providers, so you have more doctors, hospitals, and other health care professionals to select from. If you select providers outside of the plan's network, you will pay more in out-of-pocket expenses.

High-deductible plans usually have a lower premium, but you pay more health care expenses (the deductible) before the insurance company's share kicks in. You usually have the option to combine a high deductible plan with a health savings account (HSA), which allows you to pay for certain medical expenses with tax-free money.

Medicare

Medicare is the government health insurance program started in 1966 under the Social Security Administration for people 65 and older (and

CHAPTER 11

some younger people with disabilities.) If you receive Social Security benefits when you turn 65, you will be automatically enrolled in Medicare Part A. If you're not receiving Social Security benefits, you will need to sign up through the Social Security Administration.

Medicare Part A coverage includes inpatient hospital care, some limited home health services and some skilled nursing facility care. It also includes hospice care. You usually don't pay a monthly premium for Part A.

Medicare Part B coverage includes doctor visits, diagnostic services and preventive services, like flu shots. Generally, you don't pay for most preventive services if you receive the services from a doctor or health care provider who accepts Medicare. You pay a monthly premium for Part B. That premium will be automatically deducted from your check if you receive Social Security benefits. If you aren't yet receiving these benefit payments, you will get a bill.

Most people pay the standard premium. But, if your income is above a certain amount, you may pay an Income Related Monthly Adjustment Amount (IRMAA). Medicare determines if you must pay extra using the modified adjusted gross income reported on the IRS tax return you filed 2 years ago.

Medicare Part D covers prescription drugs. The monthly fee varies by plan. If you join a Medicare Advantage Plan (sometimes referred to as Part C) that monthly premium probably includes prescription drug coverage.

Medigap. This is an optional supplemental Medicare insurance. A Medigap policy would cover some of your health care costs that traditional Medicare doesn't cover, like co-payments, co-insurance and deductibles. These policies are sold by private companies.

Medicare Advantage. Medicare Advantage plans, sometimes called Medicare Part C, are an alternative to a traditional Medicare plan. Instead of having Medicare benefits administered through the traditional government program, you can get coverage through a Medicare Advantage plan. They are offered only through private insurance companies that have a contract with Medicare.

Medicare Advantage plans are required to provide at least the same level of coverage as traditional Medicare Parts A and B. However, many offer additional benefits, such as prescription drugs coverage, hearing, vision and sometimes even dental. They also generally offer wellness programs.

One final note. Medicare does not cover dental, vision or long-term care, unless you have a Medicare Advantage plan. Otherwise, you will need to get that coverage elsewhere.

Long-term care insurance

Seven out of 10 people 65 or older will need long-term care at some point. It could be from accidents, strokes, aging or chronic conditions. Nearly 6 million Americans are suffering from Alzheimer's.

By one estimate more than 60 percent of bankruptcies are caused by medical bills or issues. The question is, does long-term care insurance make sense.

A long-term care policy will help cover the cost of long-term care that is not covered by regular insurance or Medicare. It might cover your care at home, in a nursing home or at an assisted living facility. The cost varies, based on the geographic location and the level of care required, among other things. Generally, those policies pay out when the person covered is unable to perform two of the six activities of daily living such as dressing, bathing, eating, going to the bathroom, continence, getting in and out of a bed or chair and walking.

To get a sense of what that care would cost without long-term care insurance look at the chart.

Monthly Median Cost of Care

In-home care		Assisted Living		Nursing Home	
Homemaker Service	$4,481	Adult Day Care	$1,603	Semi-Private Room	$7.756
Home Health Aide	$4,576	Assisted Living	$4,300	Private Room	$8,821

Source: Genworth

Now, the question is does long-term care insurance make sense for you. There are certainly drawbacks. By the time most people recognize the need, they are near retirement age, at which time the policies are expensive. An annual policy for a 55-year-old woman would be $2,675. It would be $1,700 for a 55-year-old man and a combined $3,050 for a couple both aged 55 according to the American Association of Long-term Care Insurance. But the costs can vary widely, depending on where you live, your age, your health and type of policy. You should get your financial advisor to help when you are searching for a policy and the younger you buy the policy, the better.

The drawbacks are that, like any insurance policy, the future costs are very unpredictable, and when you stop paying you have nothing to show. There are stories of retired couples who paid for policies for years, but at some point, decided that they could no longer afford the rising premiums.

Disability Insurance

Disability insurance replaces a portion of your salary in the event you are disabled. It can be a critical source of income because most workers don't have access to income other than their wages. The Social Security Administration says that at least one in four 20-year-olds will suffer a disability for 90 days or more before they reach age 67.

If the injury doesn't happen on your job, you will not be covered by your workers' compensation, and while your health insurance will cover the cost of medical care, it won't cover your lost wages.

Most employers offer disability insurance, some at no cost to employees, some requiring a partial payment. Others offer it as an option. Even though the employee is required to pay the full cost, it is still a solid benefit because you can take advantage of your employer's group rate.

If neither is available, you can buy disability through a professional association which will offer a group rate. Or you can buy an individual policy from your insurance broker or directly from an insurance company like Guardian, Mass Mutual, Mutual of Omaha or Breeze.

Consider a disability insurance policy if you are self-employed, not covered or don't have enough disability coverage in your work. You can generally find a policy that pays 75 percent of your salary, but most have benefit limits. The annual cost is generally 1 percent to 4 percent of your annual salary, though your health, occupation and job history will probably be considered.

Short-term disability insurance covers you for a short term after an illness or injury keeps you from work, usually measured in months, generally 3 to 6 months, and covers a greater percentage of your income – up to 70 percent. Long-term disability benefits cover years, like two, five, or 20 years, or until retirement. Long term benefits cover a smaller percentage of your income, generally 40 percent to 70 percent.

Find an insurance broker

Find an insurance broker the same way you would find a financial advisor or attorney: Look for references from friends, family and colleagues or members of your house of worship. Shop around and besides looking for the ones that will offer you the best rates, make sure you are comfortable talking to him or her about your life and your needs.

An insurance broker differs from an insurance agent in that the broker represents the consumer and searches all insurers for the best policy for you at the best price. An agent generally represents one or two insurance companies. It's always best to get multiple quotes from multiple insurance companies. Brokers sell all types of insurance, and while you can save you time and money, you may have to pay a fee for their services. Most, however, are paid with commissions from the insurance companies.

12

Financial literacy is a key to growing generational wealth

CHAPTER 12

John Rogers is the founder of Ariel Investments in Chicago, where he also serves as chairman and CEO. He is also a well-known philanthropist. His legacy may be his contribution to financial literacy for Black and Brown children in Chicago, a legacy that has changed the lives of children and families on Chicago's South Side for generations to come.

Rogers saw his vision come to life as Ariel Academy, a public school that was the vision of Rogers and his good friend, former U.S. Education Secretary Arne Duncan under President Obama. Duncan worked for Rogers when the elementary school was founded 25 years ago. It has already had a huge impact on the community. Among the graduates are doctors, lawyers, entrepreneurs, and investment bankers.

"I tell people all the time that the best way to learn about investing is the way my father taught me," Rogers told me in an interview a few years back. "He gave me the money to invest in real stocks. That's the heart of what makes our program work. It's not a game."

Each class in the school, which goes from grades K through 8, has about 25 students. Much of the curriculum is like any other grade school, with classes in math, science, fine arts, music and technology. The big difference is that the school has three instructors who are dedicated to teaching financial literacy.

The financial education starts in the kindergarten and first grade, where they learn the basics of economics and personal finance using an age-appropriate curriculum. For the youngsters it may be how much it costs to buy a bike compared to a family's weekly income. They learn where money comes from and how you earn it. By the third grade the students start to learn about stocks and bonds.

But here's what's unique about the school. Each year the two kindergarten classes begin the year with $10,000 each, contributed initially by Ariel Investments. In the early grades the money is managed by Ariel. But as they get older the students actively manage the $20,000 portfolio themselves. A junior board of directors, composed of students in the 6th, 7th and 8th grades then takes over management of the money.

When the eighth-grade students graduate, that $20,000 goes back to the incoming kindergarten class. The surplus, which averages $13,000

CHAPTER 12

but has been as high as $30,000, is divided – half to the graduating students and the other half to the school. The students can then do with the money what they want, but Ariel will add another $500 if they put their earnings into a college savings fund. Ninety percent of the students chose to save for college.

This is a school that is having a huge impact on the Black community and changing lives. Students share their knowledge with the parents, and some of them change their habits along the way.

No doubt, there is a huge need for financial literacy for all ages in the Black communities across the United States, programs like the Ariel Academy that are changing lives.

According to the TIAA Institute, "the financial well-being of African Americans lags that of the U.S. population, and Whites in particular. The reasons for this gap are complex, but one area of importance in addressing it is increased financial literacy. [45]

"Financial literacy is low among many U.S. adults, including African Americans. On average, African American adults answered 38 percent of the P-Fin Index (TIAA Institute-Global Financial Literacy Excellence Center at George Washington University) questions correctly. Only 28 percent answered over one-half of index questions correctly, with 5 percent answering over 75 percent correctly.[46]"

Among the findings in the TIAA report:

- Financial literacy within the African American community is greater among men, older individuals, those with more formal education, and those with higher incomes.
- Insurance is the least understood area of personal finance among African Americans, closely followed by understanding risk, investing, and identifying information sources.
- Borrowing and debt management are the areas of highest personal finance knowledge among African Americans.
- A lack of financial resilience was more common among African Americans than Whites in 2019, before the onset of COVID-19 and its economic consequences.

- There is a strong link between financial literacy and financial wellness among African Americans. Those who are more financially literate are more likely to plan and save for retirement, to have non-retirement savings and to better manage their debt; they are also less likely to be financially fragile.

Personal finance knowledge among African Americans tends to be lower than that of Whites. On average, White adults answered 55% of the *P-Fin Index* questions correctly (Figure 2). Sixty-two percent of Whites answered over one-half of the index questions correctly, with 22% answering over 75% correctly (Figure 3). One-third of African Americans demonstrated a relatively low level of financial literacy, i.e., they answered 25% or less of the index questions correctly, compared with 16% of Whites.

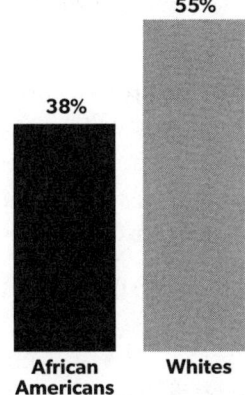

Figure 2. 2019 P-Fin Index

African American financial literacy lags that of whites

% of P-Fin questions answered correctly

Theodore Daniels, president and founder of the Society for Financial Education & Professional Development (SFE&PD) says Black parents need to talk to their children about money. "It's a generational thing," he said. "They never talked to their parents about it, so they never thought about talking to their children about it. There's a culture here that we need to address.

CHAPTER 12

"You have some parents who don't want the kids to know how the money is being used in the family," he said. "I've been promoting having an individual as well as a family budget with the children participating so they know exactly how much money is coming into the house and all the expenses associated with maintaining that household. They would know when they can't ask for something because the budget is not there."

Entrepreneur Dawn Kelly, owner of The Nourish Spot Juice Bar in Jamaica, Queens, N.Y., wholeheartedly agrees with sharing financial expenses with children. Her mother, a divorced mother with three kids, set an example that years later she would later follow with her own daughter.

"My mother would give me her check so I would know how much her check was, and she would make me write the checks out for the bills," she said. "Back then you weren't paying anything electronically, you were sending it in an envelope with a stamp.

"I would see that she had no money at the end, and I was the eldest," she said. "So that would get me not to ask her for anything. That's why I had a job from a young age, because I never wanted to hear her tell me no. And I always wanted to have my own money. I did the same thing with my daughter."

I talked to a young couple for a story I was writing for a magazine. They were in their mid-30s with a five-year-old daughter, and they were fiscally smart. They hadn't learned from their parents, but they were self-taught. He was a disciple of Dave Ramsey, a leading personal finance guru, an entrepreneur, author, and radio host.

The husband, Duane had listened to Ramsey on the radio, and then gone to his website and bought his books to learn more. "I heard him on the radio. That's my initial awareness" he said. And they closely followed his plan to save and get to be debt free. He followed the money guru's "six baby steps" and upped his 401(k) contributions from 8 percent to 15 percent. He had a Roth IRA as well.

His wife, Nadia, had been fiscally responsible and an avid saver from an early age. She saved from her summer jobs when she was a teen and went on to earn an MBA. She was self-taught as well - she started

CHAPTER 12

contributing to a 401(k) at 22 "and have been saving ever since." She had two 401(k)s, one from a previous employer.

One of their smart moves was to set up a 529 savings plan to pay for their daughter's college education. The 529 plans, which are tax advantaged, can be sponsored by states or educational institutions. There are both federal and state tax advantages, assuming you invest in a plan in the state in which you reside.

She said part of her self-education in financial planning had to do with personal experience. "It goes back to being self-educated and knowing experiences I went through," she said. "My parents didn't save enough for myself and sister to go to college. I had to fund most of my education on scholarships, grants and student loans. I graduated college and grad school with about $125,000 in loans. I knew I did not want my daughter to be in that situation."

One idea the couple wants to share: They encourage friends and families to donate to their daughter's 529 plan rather than buy toys for birthday and holiday presents. Many 529 plans are set up with a link that makes those donations from others relatively easy. The couple also has a financial planner, who happens to be a Black woman, to help them make the right financial decisions going forward.

Daniels, meanwhile, said his organizations has gone into high schools, colleges and churches to teach financial literacy. He believes that many parents don't talk finances with their children because they don't have a good grasp of money management themselves. Others may provide their children with misinformation.

He recalled a class on a college campus where he was approached by a student who asked if what his dad had told him was correct. It was not, and Daniels told him he shouldn't share that misinformation with anyone else.

In another case, closer to home, Daniels said a family member bought a used SUV and financed it for five years. When he told him about the issues with financing a used car with that many miles, he said he did it because his dad always finances a car for five years.

CHAPTER 12

"So, here you go, a generation being influenced by bad information."

One group that today is busting all kinds of stereotypes is Black athletes. Gone are the days when they would blow through millions in earnings and file for bankruptcy. Antoine Walker, for one, is now talking to young athletes and teens about his experiences and the mistakes he made.

But the new generation of athletes, like the NBA's Kevin Durant, Chris Paul and Harrison Barnes, and the NFL's Brandon Copeland, Michael Thomas and Malcolm Jenkins are not only sophisticated investors, but some are also going into schools and colleges to teach financial literacy. Copeland, for example, teaches a personal finance class as his alma mater, the University of Pennsylvania.

Several invested in Goalsetter, an app created by a Black woman entrepreneur Tanya Van Court, to teach financial literacy to young Black children. Van Court said part of her motivation for founding the site was that 90 percent of Americans lose their wealth after the third generation and 70 percent of African Americans will have a child who will fall out of the middle class. That shows how badly we need financial literacy education.

A growing number of politicians and educators also see the value of financial literacy. Twenty-one states now require students to take a class that integrates financial literacy, but only six require a student to take a standalone financial literacy class before graduation (Alabama, Ohio, North Carolina, Tennessee, Utah and Virginia).

Financial literacy advocates say there is evidence that students who are required to learn financial literacy make better financial decisions across multiple early adult-life money decisions, including how to pay for college. They also avoid payday lenders and credit card debt.

There is also a push to establish financial literacy at the college level. Why? Americans owe $1.7 trillion in student debt. Sixty-nine percent of college students took out student loans in 2019, graduating with an average debt of $29,900. Fourteen percent of the parents took out an average of $37,200 in federal parent PLUS loans.

CHAPTER 12

Black borrowers are among the group most impacted by student debt and struggle to pay after graduation. The Brookings Institution estimates that Black college graduates owe, on average, $52,726 in student debt while White college graduates owe $28,006.[47]

Another study, the National Financial Capability Study, found that most American students did not even try to figure out what their monthly payments would be before signing for the loans. About the same amount were concerned that they would have trouble keeping up with the payments.

Daniels, meanwhile, says his biggest problem with teaching financial literacy, whether it's at a Historically Black College or University or Black church, is getting people to show up for the classes. He's learned to get around that problem by taking the classes to places where the target audience has already gathered or teaching a session that the sponsoring institution makes mandatory. "Once they get there, they are happy they are there," he said.

Maya Rockeymoore Cummings, the widow of Rep. Elijah Cummings and CEO of Global Policy Solutions in Washington, D.C., says financial literacy is only one strategy in the fight against wealth disparity.

"I wouldn't say it's a major way, but it's a way (to overcome disparities). What is increased financial knowledge going to do if the bank won't lend to you.

"We need to understand that financial literacy is important for its own sake, but not necessarily to close the racial wealth gap. When more people save what they earn, that's great. But when they're earning 30 cents less on every dollar of a White person, they don't have the discretionary income necessary to compound and build their wealth."

13

Black women face unique financial challenges

CHAPTER 13

A lifetime of racial and health inequities has pushed Black Americans to the edge, at risk of growing old with declining health, low income and no savings. But Black women are especially vulnerable to both health and wealth issues as they live a lifetime in and out of the job force in low wage jobs. They are also likely to outlive their partners and are more likely to grow old alone and in poverty.

"Many Black older Americans have endured decades of overt and subtle forms of discrimination in educational, criminal justice systems, and healthcare systems as well as in jobs, housing, credit and consumer markets," said Tyson Brown, associate professor of sociology at Duke University. As a result, Black older adults have lower levels of education, income and wealth than Whites, he said.

Black Americans suffer disproportionally from eight of the top 13 top causes of death in the U.S. – heart disease, stroke, cancer, influenza and pneumonia, diabetes, HIV disease, kidney failure and homicide, says Dr. Ebony Jade Hilton, associate professor of Anesthesiology and Critical Care Medicine at University of Virginia and an outspoken critic of racial health inequities.

Black women, older Black woman in particular, suffer especially poor health, Brown says. As a result, they suffer from some of the highest levels of diabetes, hypertension, and other disabilities.

They also have the lowest levels of income and wealth, which often means they often need to continue working until later years. Yet, their health problems limit their ability to continue working. "And so, it's sort of a Catch-22, that they're often sort of put in a bind there," Brown said.

Racial and Gender Wage Disparity

"Black and Latina women are at the bottom of the barrel," said Maya Rockeymoore Cummings, the widow of Rep. Elijah Cummings and CEO of Global Policy Solutions in Washington, D.C. "Latina women are actually doing better in terms of entrepreneurship. Black women are literally at the bottom of the barrel. And that's because many of us are not only single household families but we have kids, and we're actively in debt. When you are trying to run a family, you're getting paid the least, you have the least amount to work with, in terms of building wealth."

According to a report from Morningstar[48]

- The estimated lifetime earnings of a woman with a bachelor's degree are just 60% of the estimated lifetime earnings of her male counterpart.
- Adult daughters are nearly twice as likely as adult sons to be the informal long-term caregivers of one or more parents.
- The average annual Social Security benefit collected by a 65-year-old woman is 22% less than the annual benefit collected by a 65-year-old man.

History shows us that systemic discrimination in pay and exploitation of workers based on race, class, gender can be traced all the way back to our nation's history of enslaving Africans and their descendants and the centuries of Jim Crow policies and racism that followed.

Today, Black women in the U.S. who work full time are typically paid just 63 cents for every dollar paid to White men. The wages of Black women are driven down by a number of current factors including gender and racial discrimination, workplace harassment, job segregation and lack of workplace policies that support family caregiving, which is still most often performed by women.

Median wages for Black women in the United States are $41,098 per year, compared to median wages of $65,208 annually for White, non-Hispanic men - a difference of $24,110 each year.[49]

Also, women are more likely to work part-time, have shorter careers and shorter job tenures. In addition, they continue to work in industries with lower earnings, such as service and sales/office. Even among professional workers, women are more likely to have lower earnings.[50]

The impact on savings and investments

The fact that Black women are underemployed and underpaid has an impact on their economic well-being for life. It means that many don't

CHAPTER 13

qualify for employer-sponsored 401(k) plans, and when they do, they under-contribute. They also have less savings and investments than White women.

Savings in employer-based retirement plans like 401(k)s and 403(b)s play a major role for many workers in creating a retirement savings plan. Unfortunately, Black workers, and Black women in particular, are less likely to work for employers that offer such benefits. Nearly two-thirds of White workers have a retirement savings at their workplace compared to 54% of Black workers. Most employers often contribute money to those 401(k) accounts in the form of an employer match.

Black Americans often don't participate in retirement accounts at work and then don't get the advantage of stock market growth. Only 44% of Black Americans have retirement savings accounts, with a typical balance of around $20,000, compared to 65% of White Americans, who have an average balance of $50,000, according to the Federal Reserve. And only 34% percent of African Americans own any stocks or mutual funds, compared to more than half of White people.

Single White women had an average of $56,514 in retirement savings in 2016 vs. $13,405 for single Black women.[51]

Yvonne McNair, founder and president of Captivate Marketing in New York, said a financial planner helped her get her finances in order. Growing up, her she learned a lot from her parents, but not personal finance. And she initially thought she needed to be wealthy to have a financial advisor.

Her advice to other Black women: "Save, save, save. There are so many things that you might want to purchase, or you might think you need. So just be smart about what you do spend your money on so you can save as much as possible.

"And don't do things because you think you should for appearance's sake," McNair says. "I used to have a car because I was like this helps me close deals because I looked successful. That was dumb. Don't waste money on things that don't matter. Saving is so important."

As I said earlier, a financial planner is an asset to you. You don't have to feel insecure. You don't have to be intimidated. You don't have to have all this money in the bank. If you have $5 You can start with a financial planner, and they can help you get to where you want to go. The goal of the financial planner is to help you achieve your financial goals, not to judge you, not to make you think that you aren't successful. The goal is for them to help you, so I think that's so important for people to have a financial planner.

Reliance on Social Security

Those who don't save enough for retirement often must rely on Social Security. According to the U.S. Social Security Administration, about 38 percent of minority beneficiaries rely on Social Security for 90 percent or more of their income, compared to 28 percent of White Americans.

Social Security benefits are also lower on average for African Americans because they are based on income and work history, and African Americans historically earn less at all income levels due to historic racism and discrimination.

Among African Americans receiving Social Security in 2017, 35 percent of elderly couples and 58 percent of elderly singles relied on Social Security for 90 percent or more of their income, according to the Social Security Administration. Nearly a third of older African American women depend on Social Security for nearly all their income, far higher than women in other racial and ethnic groups.

The Coronavirus pandemic has been a disaster for women

Women are more than twice as likely as men to work part time (29.4 percent vs. 15.8 percent). Working part-time means that it is less likely that the worker will receive benefits, such as paid vacation, family or medical leave, sick days, health insurance and employer-sponsored retirement plans like 401(k)s and 403(b)s.

And financial literacy expert Neale Godfrey wrote in Kiplinger's in March 2021: "In heterosexual relationships, women are more likely to be the lower earners, meaning their jobs are considered a lower priority when disruptions come along. And this disruption could last months, rather than weeks."

He said things like the pandemic magnify the inequalities faced by women. "Some women's lifetime earnings will never recover."

Black women as caregivers and the role it plays in the wealth gap

Women serve disproportionately as caregivers in the United States, and Black women play an even larger role.

For one thing, African Americans are the most likely to extend in-home care rather than relying on nursing homes or paid live-in care. Thus, Black women face the financial burden of managing a multigenerational family. The Black single mother often struggles with juggling eldercare, childcare, social life, work, and finances.

According to the Centers for Disease Control and Prevention[52], one in four African American adults are caregivers and nearly half have provided care for someone for at least two years. Sixty-one percent of those are women, of which:

- 13 percent are 65 years old or older
- 35 percent are caring for a parent or in-law
- 9 percent are caring for someone with dementia

Contributing to the large caregiving role of Black women is that Black Americans in general face a plethora of health issues. Dr. Ebony Hilton, associate professor of anesthesiology and critical care medicine at the University of Virginia, said Blacks suffer higher rates of eight of the top 13 top causes of death in the U.S. – heart disease, stroke, cancer, influenza and pneumonia, diabetes, HIV disease, kidney failure and homicide.

CHAPTER 13

Tips for Improving your financial well-being and your confidence

A good friend is writing a book encouraging women to be more confident in making financial and investment decisions. Her point was a good one. Women have no problem making some of life's most important decisions, especially when it comes to their children. They should have the same confidence when they make financial and investment decisions. They will do loads of research in picking a day care center or school. They can use that same skill set to make investment decisions.

Financial advice to help Black women improve financially does not differ substantially from the advice I would give to anyone else.

1. **Educate yourself.** According to a Federal Reserve survey, women are less comfortable making retirement investment decisions, and they show lower levels of financial literacy than men. Only 32% of women with a bachelor's degree are comfortable managing their own investments. This book's chapter on financial literacy offers advice on improving in that area. Also, the resource guide at the back of the book has a long list of books and websites that will be useful to anyone looking to gain a basic knowledge of finance.

2. **Set financial goals.** Set both short-term and long-term financial goals. Short term goals may be things like buying something personal for you, buying a car or paying a credit card down or off. Your longer-term goal may be saving for a house, your child's college tuition or building up your retirement account.

3. **Do a budget.** Most people have no idea what they spend in a month. You can thank credit cards for that. Do a budget and look at what you bring in and what your monthly expenses are. Every financial planner I talk to will tell the first thing they do when they create a financial plan for new clients is ask them to put together a budget. And most people are shocked by how they spend vs. how much they thought they were spending.

4. **Have an emergency fund.** Most people do not have the savings to cover a $1,000 emergency without using a credit

card. So, it's imperative that you save for the emergency fund before you save for anything else. There's no reason a car repair or a hiring a plumber in an emergency should put you in debt.

5. **Contribute to your 401(k).** At the very minimum contribute up to your employer's match. But it is highly recommended that you contribute more, at least 10 percent of your wages. If you are not comfortable with picking the mutual funds in your 401(k), get some professional advice.

6. **Hire a financial planner.** One of the biggest issues in getting women to connect with financial planners and invest is a trust issue, according to multiple surveys. WorthFM, a Philadelphia-based roboadvisor, says 76 percent of women felt that Wall Street does not have the best interests of consumers at heart and 91 percent said financial companies are more about selling them products than educating them about investing. While there aren't comparable surveys for Black women, you can assume the same mistrust.

One reason many Black Americans don't seek the help of a financial planner is they think they don't have enough assets. Another reason is they think the cost will be prohibitive. Neither is true. Of course, some financial planners take only high-net-worth clients, but most have no minimum income or asset requirement. At the very least, you can go to a fee-only financial planner and create a personalized financial plan.

"A financial planner is an asset to you," says McNair. "You don't have to feel insecure. You don't have to be intimidated. You don't have to think that you must have all this money in the bank. If you have $5 You can start with a financial planner, and they can help you get to where you want to go. The goal of the financial planner is to help you achieve your financial goals, not to judge you, not to make you think that you aren't successful. The goal is for them to help you, so I think that's so important for people to have a financial planner."

Business owner Dawn Kelly, who opened The Nourish Spot in Jamaica Queens, N.Y., has had a financial planner for years. She learned financial planning not as a youth growing up in New York or even in college. She learned when she worked for one of the nation's leading financial services firms.

"If you want to learn how to play golf right you will get an instructor," she said. "If you want to know how to swim, you will get an instructor. So, getting a financial advisor is no different. It's having a coach, a person that's more astute than you in the art of investing and saving."

Kelly's financial planner is a Black male who she's worked with for years. "I would much rather have my finances in the hands of capable individuals, but somebody that's familiar to me," she said.

"Basically, Black women are not in a good financial position," said Rockeymoore Cummings. "And yes, I think that there are targeted strategies that need to go into basically boosting their entrepreneurship, boosting their retirement security and boosting their opportunities to savings."

14

What if you haven't saved enough to retire

CHAPTER 14

I hear stories all the time about people who put in their retirement paperwork, and only then decided to visit a financial planner. Do I need to tell you that's a very bad idea? Because sometimes when they run the numbers, the financial planner must break the bad news that they haven't saved enough money and can't retire.

Hearing from a financial advisor that they would run out of money in 10 years is a big shock to some of them. They are prone to look at their 401(k) or other retirement account balances, and for most it's more money than they've had in their lives. But the question is, will that money last them for the rest of their lives. In many cases, the answer is no.

How much is enough?

My first book was an eBook titled "Is $1 million Enough: A Guide to Planning for and Living Through a Successful Retirement." The question put to financial planners across the United States was can you retire comfortably with savings of $1 million. One financial advisor actually said you would need $2 million. But the most common and more practical answer was: It depends.

It depends on where you live, what lifestyle you are accustomed to, how much you've saved, how much you spend each year and whether you have a budget.

Running out of money in retirement is American's biggest retirement fear across generations, according to a survey by the Transamerica Center for Retirement Studies. They found that 40 percent of the people who responded to their survey said it was their top fear.

Yet, we still aren't saving enough and don't seem to realize that the responsibility for our well-being as we age is on us, not the companies who we work for who help fund our 401(k)s.

We're at least a generation away from the time when companies provided pensions. Our fathers and grandfathers would work for the same company for 30 years and leave with a pension that provided guaranteed income for life. Today unless you are a municipal, state or federal government employee, you most likely do not have a pension.

CHAPTER 14

Companies found them too expensive and cumbersome and moved to 401(k)s and 403(b)s. Though many contribute to your 401(k), the responsibility for your life in retirement has shifted to you. It is your responsibility to contribute, and it is your responsibility to select the correct investment options within the fund to ensure that your money grows.

We have failed badly in this responsibility. Some people consider the switch to 401(k)s, a primary source of retirement funding, to be a complete failure. That's a debate that we could have for years, but it doesn't solve anything. The fact is that most of us don't get serious about retirement until we get into our 50s. And the later we wait, the harder it is to recover.

Life gets in the way

The fact is that life sometimes gets in the way. It brings me back to the woman who called me when I was doing a radio show to ask advice. A proud 50-year-old single mother had put her daughter through an Ivy League college, but she had saved nothing for her own retirement.

She was clearly behind in preparing for retirement, but she still had time to correct the situation. Many have been in this situation before and emerged with a great outlook for retirement. The people we worry most about are the ones who work into their 60s and still have virtually nothing to show for their retirement. And I'm not necessarily talking about the working poor.

Couples making $200,000 a year spend lavishly, buy new cars and big houses and take expensive vacations with no thought of what will happen when one or both can no longer work or is ready to retire. They have a lifestyle (and the debt) based on an income of $200,000 a year, and it will come as a shock when they discover that as they age, they can no longer afford to live in the lifestyle they have grown accustomed.

There are also the sad stories of the people who have lost a spouse and are not prepared to lose 50 percent of their annual income. One financial planner told me a story about a middle-aged client who lost her husband to Covid-19. She was not prepared to live on half of the income she was accustomed to. Her question: "What should I do." The answer is she can downsize or face a possibly dramatic change in her lifestyle.

It happens more frequently to retirement-age clients who don't think about what will happen if one of the spouses passes, even if they are already retired.

A good financial planner will tell you that it's never too late to start saving for retirement. Believe me, that planner is being nice. The later you show up in a financial planner's office, the more difficult it will be for a financial advisor to be able to help you recover.

There are, however, success stories of people who have done what they needed and more than made up for the years of not saving. One couple I know doubled up on their savings for the 10 years before their planned retirement to catch up. They were so committed they ended saving even more than their financial advisor recommended by the time they were ready for their retirements.

Here are some things you need to think about to get your savings on track.

Work longer

The first thought many have is to work longer. There are huge advantages to continuing to work into your 60s or in your 70s.

According to a survey by Voya Financial, 54 percent of workers across generations planned to work in retirement. That includes 54 percent of Baby Boomers, 60 percent of Gen Xers and 49 percent of Millennials. And nearly a third of today's retirees said they receive at least some income from working.

A United Income survey said twice as many Americans over 65 are working today compared with 1985.[53] The U.S. Bureau of Labor Statistics says the numbers will continue to grow, estimating that 13 million Americans 65 and older will be in the workforce in 2024.

The typical worker has saved $50,000 for retirement, according to the Transamerica Center for Retirement Studies, but for people earning less than $50,000 a year that number drops to $3,000.

CHAPTER 14

The average 401(k) balance by age

How much Americans have in their 401(k) savings as of the fourth quarter of 2020

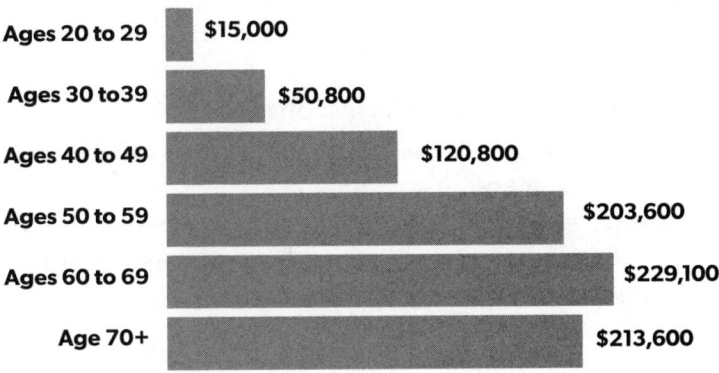

Ages 20 to 29	$15,000
Ages 30 to 39	$50,800
Ages 40 to 49	$120,800
Ages 50 to 59	$203,600
Ages 60 to 69	$229,100
Age 70+	$213,600

The average 401(k) contribution by age

How much Americans are contributing to their 401(k) as of the fourth quarter of 2020

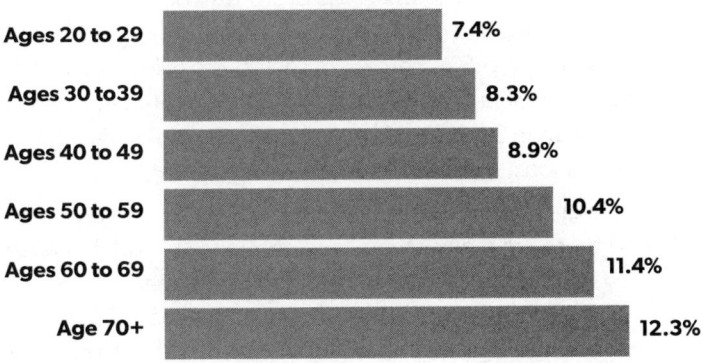

Ages 20 to 29	7.4%
Ages 30 to 39	8.3%
Ages 40 to 49	8.9%
Ages 50 to 59	10.4%
Ages 60 to 69	11.4%
Age 70+	12.3%

Source: Fidelity

The point of these charts is that, even people with 401(k)s are not saving nearly enough for a comfortable retirement. And also keep in mind that the average Social Security check in 2021 was only about $1,543 a month.

There are certainly Baby Boomers who can't wait to retire, especially those with physically or emotionally stressful professions. However, some older Americans are choosing to stay in their jobs or find new challenges that will keep them engaged.

CHAPTER 14

We are working later in life for three reasons:

- **We're living longer.** In 1970 life expectancy for people who reached 65 was 78 for men and 82 for women. Today if a man and women reach 65, their life expectancies are 84 and 86, respectively.
- **Jobs in general are a lot less physical.**
- **People in their 60s are much more active and in better physical shape.**
- **Since people are living long, they may have to work longer just to remain independent and support themselves financially.**

There are three huge advantages to continuing to work, even if it's part-time or consultant work.

1. **You will continue to earn income.** If you are unprepared for retirement, you'll need to continue to bring in income for living expenses. There are lots of stories about 80-year-old grandmothers and grandfathers working in Walmart or Home Depot. In the U.S. 9 percent of seniors are living in poverty. Those numbers are higher among women, people over 80 years old and Black and Hispanics, according to United Health Foundation's America's Health Rankings.

   There are people who work late in life because they must, and there are many others who continue to work because they want to. For these people, the additional income is a luxury rather than a necessity. These people have found that they want and need something to do or a place to go after they retire, even if it is part-time work. They work because they enjoy it.

   Warning: If you collect Social Security benefits before full retirement age, your benefits are reduced by $1 for every $1 you earn over the limit. Once you reach full retirement age, there is no limit on the amount of money you can earn and still receive your full Social Security benefit.

CHAPTER 14

2. **Your retirement savings can continue to grow.** One of the biggest benefits of continuing to work past retirement age is that your retirement nest egg can continue to grow and provide you with returns because you are not making withdrawals or are taking out less than you would if you were not working.

Let's start with an example. John Johnson officially retired from his job as social worker for a non-profit. When he retired at 62, he was earning $75,000 a year and had $250,000 in his 403(b)-retirement account. John is divorced, and his two children have already graduated from college and started their work lives. John's mortgage is about $1,200 a month, but it will be paid off in three years. He figures he can live on expenses of about $35,000 a year, including the mortgage.

He can earn up to $35,000 as a substitute teacher in his city's schools. If it works out, he will cover his expenses and will not have to touch his retirement savings account, which has been growing by 8 percent a year without any withdrawals.

With compound interest his investment account will grow to $314,926 in just three years. If he works till 70 without making major withdrawals, he will see his account grow nearly double to $462,733.

We've already discussed longevity and the challenges it poses. Though Black Americans' longevity is less than Whites, it is not uncommon for our parents and grandparents to live well into their 80s and 90s.

3. **You continue to be active, both physically and mentally.** According to a report from the Harvard Medical School several studies have linked working in retirement to better health and longevity.[54] According to that report, a study of over 83,000 adults over 15 years found that people who worked past 65, compared to people who retired, were three times more likely to report being in good health and half as likely to have serious health problems like cancer and heart disease. "Other studies have linked working past retirement age with a reduced risk of dementia and heart attacks.

CHAPTER 14

One final note (and warning) about planning to work in retirement. Many things will make it difficult for many of us to work into our 60s and 70s. According to the Employee Benefits Research Institute (EBRI), 80 percent of pre-retirees plan to work in retirement, but only 28 percent do.[55] Three quarters of those surveyed planned on those wages being least a partial source of income in retirement. And the median age of retirees is 62, but most Americans plan to work till 65. Four in 10 workers had to retire earlier than expected.

People retire early for a variety of reasons. Most of them are health or disability related. Some simply cannot perform the required work as they age, especially blue collar works. Others can no longer deal with the daily stress. And others lose their jobs because of layoffs or corporate restructuring.

Life doesn't always agree with your plans. Remember, most people stop working because they must. Poor health is a primary reason. But many others find themselves furloughed or fired from their jobs, ruining their plans to work into their 60s and 70s. And unfortunately, many of those who are forced from their jobs are unable to find work because of their age. Age discrimination is very real in America today.

Consider a reverse mortgage

Just like it sounds, a reverse mortgage is a loan that is basically the opposite of a home mortgage. Instead of you paying the bank, you receive payments from the lender. There are positives and negatives. And some financial planners only recommend them as a last resort to seniors and retirees who need the money. After some early problems and abuses, the loans have, however, become more respectable in recent years.

A homeowner 62 or older with a considerable amount of equity in his or her home can borrow against that equity and receive fixed monthly payments, a lump sum or a line of credit. The entire amount of the loan becomes due when the homeowner dies, sells the home or moves away. The advantage is that homeowners can get access to much-needed cash if their net worth is tied up in their homes.

CHAPTER 14

The amount of money available will depend on the age of the borrower (the age of the youngest borrower if it is a married couple), the home value and current interest rates.

The disadvantages are that the loans can be complex and costly, and in the past have been plagued by scams. Perhaps a bigger drawback to the loans is they effectively rob the homeowners' children and grandchildren of much-needed generational wealth when the home is sold, and the loan is repaid.

How it works

Mrs. James is a widow who has lived in her home for 30 years. She has paid off her mortgage, and her home is valued at $250,000. Her problem is that she receives only $1,500 a month in Social Security and has no other income.

According to one online mortgage calculator, Mrs. James could be eligible for a reverse mortgage amount of $73,900 after closing costs and a fixed-rate loan, which she could take as a lump sum or receive a monthly payment of $1,093 a month for life or $1,223 for the next 20 years.

The short-term advantage for Mrs. James is clear. She can nearly double her monthly income. She can qualify even with no income, and she does not need good credit. And the proceeds are not taxable and generally won't affect Social Security or Medicare payments.

The Federal Trade Commission warns you to be wary of sales pitches for reverse mortgages.

"A salesperson isn't likely to be the best guide for what works for you. This is especially true if he or she acts like a reverse mortgage is a solution for all your problems, pushes you to take out a loan, or has ideas on how you can spend the money from a reverse mortgage.[56]

You must make sure that the reverse mortgage is enough to cover property taxes, homeowners' insurance and home maintenance. Failure to stay current in any one can cause the lender to force payment of the entire loan.

CHAPTER 14

Abuses and foreclosures plagued the loans initially, especially among African Americans, but the government cracked down with new rules and regulations. Still, a USA TODAY report in 2019 outlined continued problems.

These elderly homeowners were wooed into borrowing money through the special program by attractive sales pitches or a dire need for cash – or both. When they missed a paperwork deadline or fell behind on taxes or insurance, lenders moved swiftly to foreclose on the home. Those foreclosures wiped out hard-earned generational wealth built in the decades since the Fair Housing Act of 1968.[57]

Downsize

It's not a pleasant thought, but it's not uncommon for a married couple to lose 50 percent of their income when one spouse dies. Since women live longer than men, you are more likely to see this impact as a widow.

Suddenly a couple receiving two Social Security checks is receiving one check. Even if both were still working, the impact is the same: Income is reduced by 50 percent.

The problem is in no way limited to losing a spouse. I've said many times in earlier chapters that Americans are ill prepared for retirement. Most of us have not saved nearly enough. And that trip to the financial advisor results in the realization that you'll run out of money in 10 years.

If there were no other sources of income, the choices are either a change in lifestyle or to downsize. That smaller home or apartment could mean a dramatic decrease in housing and other expenses.

Cut expenses

This goes back to the advice about creating a budget. As hard as it might be to cut expenses, there are ways to do it. Consider:

- **Start by keeping track of your spending.** People are usually shocked when they write down what they spend on a weekly or monthly basis. They usually grossly underestimate their expenses.
- **Avoid using credit cards for everything.** Many Millennials don't even carry cash these days. It's easy to charge, but you don't really see what you spend and what you spend it on unless your closely study your credit card statements.
- **Pay off credit card balances monthly.** Credit card debt is some of the worst debt you can imagine. Interest rates average in the double digits. Paying the minimum payment on credit card debt is a huge financial No-No.
- **Reduce your dining and entertainment budget.** I get it. People get busy and don't have time to cook. But eating out just a couple of times a week can be expensive.
- **Cut back on family vacations.** Some travel experts estimate that a visit to Disney World for a family of four will cost about $5,000, but some estimates go much higher. It becomes a problem if the cost is put on credit cards. Maybe the trip becomes a special occasion vacation instead of an annual vacation.
- **Review your insurance policies to see if there are less expensive options**
- **Refinance your home**
- **Put off that new car for another year or two**
- **Delay that home improvement project for a year**
- **Keep your old-model smart phone for another year**
- **Pay off high-interest credit cards**

Boost savings

- Set short-term and long-term savings goal
- Increase the percentage of your pay that goes into your 401(k). Some plans offer automatic increases, i.e., it will go from 5 percent to 6 percent after a year.

- When you receive pay increases automatically boost your retirement plan contributions.
- Set savings goals
- Make saving automatic. Most banks and credit unions offer free transfers from checking to savings accounts. Pay yourself first. Transfer $20, $50 or $100 a month into an account other than your checking account that you don't have easy access to.
- Bank your tax return rather than using it to pay bills or splurge.
- If you are not eligible for a 401(k) open an IRA. Companies like Charles Schwab, Fidelity and Vanguard make it easy to open accounts and set up monthly contributions of as little as $25 a month.

15

Don't let your kids (or any other members of your family) wreck your financial plan

CHAPTER 15

There's a story that has stuck with me over the years. A financial planner I talked to told me about one of his former clients who continuously sent large sums of money to her grown grandson whenever he needed it, which was often. She continued to do so even after he warned her repeatedly that she was putting her retirement savings in danger. She was not a wealthy woman.

Unfortunately, this story does not have a happy ending. In fact, I don't know the ending. The financial advisor could not tell me how the story ended because his client drew down her assets and the account was eventually closed. He then lost track of her.

Many people will do virtually anything for their children or grandchildren, even when it's to their own detriment. And sometimes those family members are so inconsiderate they don't even consider the financial consequences on their parents and grandparents.

One college student told his middle-class family that it was their fault that they were struggling to help him pay his tuition – they should have done a better job saving.

In another case, an adult married woman ran up an enormous amount of credit card debt. She was so determined to keep the debt from her husband that she threatened suicide if her mother did not give her the money to pay off the debt. The worst part of this story was that her husband was very well off, and her mother would have had to basically gut her retirement savings to give her daughter the money.

This story does have a relatively happy ending. The mother shared the story with her financial advisor, who encouraged her to tell her husband. When the daughter finally told her husband about her credit card debt, he paid it off without hesitation. No word on whether the daughter's selfishness has had a long-term impact on her relationship with her elderly mother.

Whether it's a raiding your retirement to send a child to college, supporting your children after they graduate or supporting your adult children when they divorce and return home, they can all cause irreparable harm to your retirement lifestyle and your long-term finances – unless you have a plan and a budget to help you deal with the consequences. And sometimes that involves some hard decisions.

CHAPTER 15

Should you sacrifice your retirement savings to pay for your children's education?

Seven out of ten parents plan to use at least a part of their retirement savings to pay for their children's college tuition.[58] The average cost of college tuition and fees in the 2020-2021 academic year was $9,687 at a ranked, in-state public college and $35,087 for a private college, according to U.S. News & World Report.

To emphasize the sacrifices parents are willing to make for their children:

- Fifty-three percent of parents in a T. Rowe Price survey said saving for college is a higher priority than saving for retirement.
- Sixty-eight percent said they would be willing to delay their retirement to pay for their children's college education and 24 percent said they had already used retirement funds for that purpose.[59]

Students at historically Black colleges and universities (HBCUs) rely more heavily on government loans and borrow significantly higher amounts to pay for college according to the United Negro College Fund (UNCF).[60]

- 80 percent of students at HBCUs take out loans vs. 55 percent of non-HBCU students
- 25 percent of HBCU graduates take out loans of $40,000 or more vs. 6 percent of non-HBCU grads
- 71 percent of HBCU students are low-income students vs 39 percent at non-HBCUs.

Here's something every parent should keep in mind. You can take out a loan for college, but you cannot take out a loan for retirement. The point is that you can't make up for your lack of savings after you retire. We've already discussed what happens if you don't save enough for retirement in earlier chapters.

Understandably, many parents don't want to see their kids graduate college saddled with thousands of dollars in student loan debt. But it's not a good idea to choose tuition savings over saving for retirement. As I've said repeatedly already, we are already not saving enough for our retirement. At the same time, we are living longer and paying more for health care as we age.

Think about the threat of running out of money 10 years into your retirement and being forced to subsist on Social Security. Then you will likely be a burden to those same children you were trying to protect from debt.

There are other options:

529 Plans. We discussed these tuition savings plans in the earlier chapter on saving and investing. A 529 plan is a savings plan that is designed to encourage savings for future tuition costs for your children or grandchildren. The plans, which are tax advantaged, can be sponsored by states or educational institutions. There are two types of 529 plans: prepaid tuition plans and education savings plans. They are offered by all 50 states and the District of Columbia. Prepaid tuition plans are offered by many colleges and universities. There are both federal and state tax advantages, assuming you invest in a plan in the state in which you reside.

Grants. Colleges, states, the federal government, foundations and non-profit organizations all hand out grants that in most cases do not have to be repaid. Some are based on income; others are based on the student's academic record or achievement. Still others are aimed at minority students headed for certain careers. Students received $140.9 billion in grant aid in the 2019-2020 academic year. The average was $14,940 for undergraduate students and $27,310 for graduate students.[61]

Private Scholarships. There are literally thousands of scholarships offered by private groups, foundations, trade groups, associations and community groups. Some are offered by groups encouraging students to pursue certain careers, such as finance, journalism or medicine.

Loans. We've talked extensively about student loans and student loan debt, especially the huge debt facing Black students when they graduate. Parents and students are trying desperately to reduce the debt load students face when they graduate. Students and parents can reduce the burden on both parent and student with the other options listed above.

Part-time employment or work-study jobs. The U.S. Department of Education reports that 43 percent of undergrad students and 81 percent of part-time students worked at least part time.

Boomerang Kids

Like most of my Baby Boomer friends, I never returned home after college. By the time I graduated college I was married and working more than 225 miles from my mother's home.

Things are different today, partly the result of helicopter parents and partly the result of today's economics, primarily school loan debt, which has had a huge impact on Black students especially. Student loan debt has reached $1.7 billion, or an average of $38,000.

According to one survey, 50 percent of young Millennials (22-28 years old) planned to return home after college graduation. Seven in 10 planned to stay close to home for college.[62] Fifty-six percent of parents in a Country Financial survey said they would go into debt to pay for their children's' education. A T Rowe Price survey found that 74 percent of parents prioritize their children's education over their own retirement.

It's clear that most college grads return home to cut costs, but that also increases costs for their parents, especially if the children don't contribute financially to the household budget.

According to a survey by Porch.com, the average cost of housing an adult child at home was $459 a month. "One reason for that cost could be that most boomerang kids aren't paying to reside with their parents. Just 43 percent of parents with adult children at home said their kids pay rent, though 83 percent said their children pitched in in other ways, like performing chores."[63]

The key to managing your finances when your children return home, according to financial planners, is communication. Parents and children need to have an open and honest conversation about financial expectations. That discussion should take place early and include whether and how much the children can/should contribute to household expenses or if they will contribute in other ways. This is also the time to discuss how long the children will live at home.

Whether to charge your adult children can be an emotional discussion, but it's one you should have. Not every parent can support their grown children, and some may be reluctant to discuss their finances with their children. Other parents are comfortable with having their children not pay rent if their children are savings towards a goal, like homeownership or deposits for rent.

Supporting children who don't live at home

Even when they don't live at home, millions of parents are helping to support their children who don't live at home, and you can again attribute this to the parents' concern for the huge student loan burden that many are carrying. Parents subsidize rents and mortgages, pay cell phone bills and car payments, even if they've been out of college for years. A colleague continued to pay his children's cell phone bills well into their 20s and got push-back when he urged them to pay their own bills, which he eventually did.

A Credcards.com survey said half of parents with adult children helped their children financially during the coronavirus pandemic and nearly 80 percent used money they would have used in their own personal finances. The most common reasons were food (47 percent), housing (33 percent) cellphone payments (27 percent) and car payments (23 percent).[64]

Adult children with their own kids returning home after a divorce or job loss

What can be an even bigger burden is when adult kids who have lived independently for years return home after a trauma like a job loss or divorce. Sometimes they arrive with kids in tow.

CHAPTER 15

The two biggest impacts, besides the whole household dynamic changing, are dramatically increased expenses and the impact on retirement, especially when most people already know they have not saved enough for retirement.

Again, open communication is the key. If they are working, will they contribute to the household budget? Will they help with household chores? What are childcare arrangements (if necessary)? Is this a temporary living arrangement or are they thinking longer term? To what degree do they need your financial help?

At this point you should know what you can do realistically to help. If you want to help, the key is to not overextend yourself financially and try to do it without impacting your retirement savings.

When family members and friends ask you for loans or to co-sign a loan

Nearly half of adults who loaned to friends or family reported negative outcomes, according to a Bankrate.com survey.[65] Thirty-seven percent said they lost money and 21 percent experienced a damaged relationship.

Similarly, 45 percent who co-signed a loan said they experienced a negative consequence: 20 percent said their credit score suffered and 18 percent said they lost money.

Avoiding miscommunication, damaged relationships and financial pain

They key to helping our family members is to do it without long-term financial damage.

- Much of that damage can be avoided by good honest communication. Also, a budget and a financial plan will help. Start saving for both your retirement and college tuition early, even if it's just a few dollars. Just get into the savings habit.

Get a financial planner to help you achieve your goals.
- If your children return home, whether it's after college or years later, a sometimes-uncomfortable conversation is necessary. Set savings goals for the children. Outline your expectations for work or a job search and whether you expect them to pay some expenses.
- Avoid co-signing a loan for children or friends. There's a good chance you will be penalized financially or with an impact on your credit. That loan will count on your credit score, whether your child keeps it current or not.
- And finally, as ridiculous as it may sound, if you are determined to loan a friend or relative money, write up a legal document. A friend told me his mother made him sign a loan agreement and pay 8 percent interest when he needed a loan. It doesn't just help ensure that you will be repaid, it also builds character and responsibility in your children. (He repaid the loan on time and with interest.)

16

Is starting a business a part of your financial plan? It may be harder than you thought

CHAPTER 16

Dawn Kelly was 52 when her new boss at a financial services company called her into a one-on-one meeting where she was unexpectedly and unceremoniously fired. In HR terms, she was being downsized and her job was being eliminated.

She received a severance package, but the anger and resentment still lasted for months.

"I was home, and to be honest I was just crying every day, feeling like a loser and a failure," she said. "I went on like one job interview, and I walked out of it. I wasn't ready to put my life in someone else's hands, because (her former boss) was so cavalier when he eliminated my job. It really was kind of devastating."

It took her daughter to bring her out of her funk when she asked her: 'Could you find my mother? Because my mother's a fighter. I don't know who you are.' "And that challenge kind of put a fire underneath my butt."

Her daughter's challenge and watching a CNN story on a new juice bar opening in Manhattan led Kelly to her journey as an entrepreneur. "I went out with my daughter, and I saw a storefront that said, DK upholstery. My name is Dawn Kelly. Today I'm in that place, and my store has been thriving since that moment."

Kelly used money from her severance package and withdrawals from her 401(k) to fund the business and to pay living expenses through the startup.

After five years, The Nourish Spot in Jamaica, Queens, New York, which offers juices and healthy eating choices, is earning a profit. Kelly can see paying herself a salary soon.

Many of us dream of working for ourselves. That's not a bad thing. But you need to go into it with your eyes wide open. If you think working for someone else is difficult, working for yourself will probably be even harder. The failure rate for new small businesses is atrocious. The failure rate for new Black businesses is even worse.

Today, there are 2.6 million Black businesses in the U.S., 35 percent of them owned by Black women. Those owned by Black women earn significantly less than businesses owned by White women. Also, Black businesses receive less business financing and at higher interest rates.

And 44 percent of Black business owners use their own cash to start their businesses.[66]

According to the U.S. Bureau of Labor Statistics, 20 percent of small businesses fail in the first year; 30 percent fail in the first two years; 50 percent fail after 5 years; and by the 10th year, 70 percent have failed.

Kelly is one of the rare success stories. Most Black businesses are one person operations, and, like most small businesses, most of them don't make it. According to Bloomberg, 80 percent of Black businesses fail in the first 18 months. The biggest reasons: they are generally underfunded, there is usually not a true vision, or a business plan and they have not done enough research.

The Paycheck Protection Program highlighted these financing inequities. By some estimates, the number of Black-owned businesses dropped by 40 percent during the pandemic shutdowns. Many will not see the light of day. And because many Black businesses have shaky financials, have little access to capital and a lack a relationship with banks of any size, many were not able to take advantage of the PPP loans.

Here is some advice on how to survive as a Black business for more than 18 months.

Make sure you have the funding to survive until your business can generate sufficient capital

Most small businesses, especially Black-owned small businesses, fail because they run out of money. Because Black businesses are undercapitalized, they are devastated by economic downturns brough on by events like the Great Recession and the Covid-19 pandemic hit.

"There are 2.6 million Black businesses in America," says Roland Martin, political commentator, entrepreneur, and host of #Roland Martin Unfiltered, a daily digital news program. "About 2.5 million of them have one employee. They are sole proprietorships, so they are not actually businesses with capacity. The problem is any slight shift in the economy can be devastating."

"Our Black businesses don't have the reserves to be able to weather these types of storms (like Covid-19)," said Martin. "So, when it hits, it obliterates."

Historically, it has been extraordinarily difficult for Black- and women-owned businesses to obtain bank financing, even with a strong business plan.

Venture capitalists tend to look for existing patterns of success before they will make an investment, according to Fast Company Magazine. So, even before they reach the stage of pitching a company, Black and minority would-be entrepreneurs have a lack of access to capital that would allow them to get their ventures off the ground. Also, most Black entrepreneurs do not have access to a network that can provide them with a type of investment known as a "Friends and Family." As a result, they're rarely able to make that crucial first step toward jump-starting a business.[67]

Though Kelly used her severance package and 401(k) loans to get her business on the ground, many financial advisors recommend against using your retirement savings to start a business, and I would agree, especially if you are trying to start a business in your later years. The survival rate for Black businesses is so dismal, the older you are the less likely you would be able to recover financially to have a comfortable retirement.

Charlie Partridge, a business consultant and retired corporate minority supplier development executive, says since Blacks don't have the inherited wealth or networks that White business owners have access to, we have to look at other alternatives. "If you don't have some kind of healthy savings or a financial cushion, it's really difficult for a person to start a business unless they have a spouse that can maybe carry some of the load as they are starting to develop and build their business," she said. "You either have to have some money or a damn good strategy."

Talk to a financial advisor

Nicolas Abrams, a Certified Financial Planner and president of AJW Financial Partners in Baltimore, Maryland, says he generally advises against funding a new venture with money from your retirement savings because the world has changed. People don't work for a company for 30 years and get a gold watch and a pension. The 401(k) is often the

CHAPTER 16

only money other than Social Security that you must live through what could be a long retirement.

But it may work for some. Some people will use their retirement savings even if it is a risky venture. But if you do, Abrams said, make sure you talk to a financial professional first. There are business strategies and tax strategies that you might not be aware of that could save you a lot of pain, heartache, and taxes in the future. Much depends on your situation.

The only person who is going to honestly tell you whether you can afford to take the entrepreneurial plunge and your chances of success is your financial planner or advisor, whether it's borrowing from your 401(k) or using other savings.

Yvonne McNair, founder and president of Captivate Marketing in New York said she found her financial advisor's advice to be invaluable when she left the corporate job and went out on her own. Now she has 10 employees and dozens of subcontractors across the United States.

"Finances were never my thing," she said. "I'm more of a creative. I was a little intimidated to be quite honest, because in my mind I thought that you had to have all this money before getting a financial planner instead of understanding that a financial planner can help you achieve your financial goals. I've been in business for 13 years and have had one for half of those years."

She said her financial advisor helped her put a better structure in place for her business and allowed her to be more profitable and understand how to save. And just as importantly, she helped her put business systems in place.

Have a realistic business plan

Most Black businesses fail because they are undercapitalized, sure, but many run out of money either because they did not have a business plan, or their business plan was flawed.

Black business failure is often related to the "poor business plan" case. A business plan can be based on an inaccurate market study, it can overstate the potential market share that the new business might garner over the course of time. Or the prices being charged by that business might not with steeped in reality. These incorrect assumptions may lead that new entrepreneur to believe that the financing required to start and sustain the business is less than what will be required. As a result, the revenue generated won't be sufficient to sustain the business.[68]

Do your research and understand your market

Personally, my dream business used to be owning an old used bookstore with shelves upon shelves of dusty old books that I could read while I wait for customers. That's my dream business, but luckily, I recognized early that it would not a very profitable one. Books and reading are my hobby, not a business. Many prospective entrepreneurs start a business that they have dreamed about for years, and they fail to understand what market that their business will be catering to.

I know artsy type people who wanted to concentrate on the softer side of business and had no interest in the "business side" of entrepreneurship. That's a disaster waiting to happen. I saw one very promising partnership break up because of that – one partner was business-centric, and the other was 100 percent creative, and they could never merge both approaches. You need to understand at least the basics of business - taxes, accounting, sales and marketing. And if you don't understand finances, find someone who does.

Partridge, the retired small business consultant, says other than financing, the biggest challenges Black start-ups face is that they typically go for the "low-hanging fruit" when they decide to start a business. "And the low hanging fruit is always the most competitive businesses with the smallest margins," she said.

She told the story of one Black entrepreneur who failed four times in starting his business until he found success with his fifth try. He learned the lesson of the low hanging fruit," she said. "That's why he kept failing, because his competition was so fierce where the margins were so low." His fifth try was in a very specialized market in the technology industry, "and he grew tremendously and profitably."

CHAPTER 16

Never stop learning

"I've not stopped learning," said Kelly. "I think it is the key to my success. I take every class that I possibly could on entrepreneurship, cash flow, forecasting, hiring, and cost of goods sold. These were all terms that I was not familiar with before. "

McNair echoed the importance of continuing to educate yourself. "Nowadays, you can find YouTube videos, you can find free courses," said McNair. "There are so many things out there that you can find. Goldman Sachs has some programs like that that are free to entrepreneurs. There are so many resources out there. Take advantage of all the resources."

She said she reads and takes classes constantly. "The world changes, so I always want to be fresh and understand what's going on in the world."

Partridge cited a study done by Howard University students in Washington, D.C. in the late 1960s at the request of Abraham Venable, the first head of the U.S. Commerce Department's Office of Minority Business Enterprise. As the city became more integrated, Black people left Black-owned cleaners to go to White-owned cleaners. He wanted to know why. It turned out that the White cleaners charged less. They had technology that reduced the cost of cleaning clothes considerably – technology that the owners of the Black cleaners didn't even know existed. (It's doubtful, however, that they could have afforded the new technology even if they knew about it.)

CHAPTER 16

You may need to lean on friends and family to staff up, but be careful

Black entrepreneurs, like many racial minorities and immigrants, tend to rely heavily on friends and family for staffing. That can be wonderful. But if you've ever watched a popular TV show called Bar Rescue on the Paramount Network, you'll know that host John Taffer has saved countless bars that have been run into the ground by friends and relatives of the owners. Sometimes it's the owners themselves who are the problem.

Even if it's your best friend, your spouse or your sibling, if you want them involved in your business, you need to make sure that their knowledge and skillset matches the job that you assign them to do.

Find a mentor and talk to other entrepreneurs about their successes and mistakes

"Talk to people who are doing what you want to do," McNair says. "Get advice from those people who understand some of the challenges. So don't be afraid to reach out to people within your industry, people who are doing what you want to do. I think that's very critical.

"Surround yourself with some smart people," she said. "I have my little personal board of advisors, where I can bounce things off. And if you don't know those people, try and find those people. Most people are willing to help if you ask."

My wife, Sheila Brooks, owns a multi-cultural advertising agency in Washington, D.C. She has been in business for 30 years, and created a board of advisors for her company, SRB Communications, that met quarterly. It consisted of bankers, business consultants, attorneys and media professionals. She gave them a small honorarium for attending meeting, but they served in a voluntary capacity because they admired her drive and ambition and wanted to help her company grow.

CHAPTER 16

It's all about capacity

"We have to have real analyses of types of businesses that we have," said Martin. "As long as we are just a dry cleaners or tax service, it comes to capacity. You will not hear me say we need more Black business. We need more Black businesses with capacity. That is the fundamental problem we have. We do not have capacity. We are not seeing our businesses grow form one employee to 5, to 10, to 30 and seeing revenue grow from $1 million to $2 million to $4 million, to $20 million.

"We have to have Black businesses that by their nature grow and are able to achieve capacity," he said. "That is our stumbling block."

Getting Help

U.S. Small Business Administration (SBA) Small Business Development Centers

These Centers provide management assistance to current and potential small business owners by offering expertise provided by people recruited from professional and trade associations, the legal and banking communities, colleges and universities, chambers of commerce and the Service Corps of Retired Executives (SCORE). They assist with financial, marketing, production, organization, engineering and technical problems. They make special efforts to reach minority entrepreneurs, socially and economically disadvantaged groups, women, veterans and the disabled.

SCORE (Service Corps of Retired Executives)

Score fosters business development through mentoring and education. The mentors are generally successful business owners and corporate executives who volunteer their time and expertise and have tools and resources that are specially geared toward women entrepreneurs. There is also a SCORE for Black Entrepreneurs.

National Minority Supplier Development Council (NMSDC)

The organization matches its 12,000 minority business members with corporations who might purchase their products and services. Its nearly 1,500 corporate members includes many of the nation's largest corporations. Besides its national office in New York City, the Council has two dozen affiliated regional councils.

17

Marriage, divorce, and communication

CHAPTER 17

Money is one of the top reasons for stress in a marriage. It is also one of the top reasons for divorce. That includes people who have money as well as those who don't.

But financial planners will tell you that one of the best ways to take the financial stress out of your life – and your marriage – is to have a financial plan that both partners buy into and are committed to.

In virtually every marriage there is one partner who handles the finances. Logically, that makes sense: A couple shares household duties and each does what they are best suited for. But both partners need to at least have a discussion on finances on a regular basis.

This, however, is where many couples fall short. More often than you may guess the partners have little or no conversations about finances.

Twenty percent of people keep and manage their money separately from their partners, according to the Couples and Money survey by Policygenius, an online insurance marketplace. Even more (24%) don't share any major financial accounts, including a checking, savings, credit card or mortgage account. And nearly 30% of couples in the survey didn't even know each other's salaries.[69]

Financial planners and counselors say that without financial transparency relationships can and do run into trouble. And the Policygenius survey proved them right. Among couples who don't manage money together, 20% said they planned to leave their partner due to financial problems.: Only 4% of the couples who handle finances together said they planned to leave due to their partner's money issues.

One reason people don't share financial information is that they are getting married later. The Policygenius survey supports this trend: 54.3% of couples who live together without kids manage money separately, while only 17.4% of couples who are married without kids do.

I hear stories all the time about spouses who have never met their financial planner because they left that for the other partner to do. Imagine what it would be like to have the stress of a funeral and burial while at the same time you're trying to figure out where your savings and investment accounts are, who are the layers and financial advisors and what your financial situation is.

This happens, and probably a lot more often that you think. It's imperative that both partners are involved in financial and investment decisions. And it's important that both partners know financial advisors, CPAs and attorneys. One partner handling all the meetings and decisions is a recipe for disaster. And a divorce is even worse.

Couples and communication

Even if you take finances out of the equation, communications can be a huge issue in a marriage. Without getting deep into the psychology behind couples' communication issues, let's focus on why communication is imperative in a relationship.

First, spouses need to discuss finances weekly. Both need to understand what bills need to be paid, what income is coming in and what, if anything is going into savings. Couples may avoid this because often financial conversations can cause stress, especially if you have one who is a spendthrift and one who is a saver. There needs to be compromise to avoid potential friction.

"It's very important to talk about finances, but it's one of the hardest things for people to talk about," said Nicholas Abrams, a Certified Financial Advisor (CFP) and president of AJW Financial Partners in Baltimore, Maryland.

Usually one spouse handles the finance, usually the one best suited for it, he says. But if something happens to that spouse, the surviving spouse is left in the dark – they have no idea where anything is or how to catch up with their financial situation. "That is a devastating experience," he said. "You are going through a loss. You are going through a mourning while you're trying to figure out the bills, which bills are paid, how are they paid and from which account. It's a nightmare, and I've seen spouses have to go through that."

Abrams says he's seen the surviving spouse pull out a list on a sheet of yellow paper and say, this is all he or she left. I have no idea where anything is. "So, it's very important to have that conversation about what's going on with the money. It helps financially if something happens, and it helps a healthy marriage to have that communication."

It's doubly important that both partners know the financial advisor or financial planner. Even though they recommend against it, many advisors say that often only one spouse comes in for a meeting. The other has not only not met the financial representative but doesn't even know his or her name.

One advisor told me of the shock when one of his clients bought in his wife and she discovered that if he died, she would be facing dire financial consequences. The husband was embarrassed, but he worked to fix the situation as best he could.

One of the first things a financial advisor will ask you during your introductory visit is what does retirement look like for you. Both spouses need to answer. They need to be on the same page about retirement. But I hear all the time about one couple's vision of retiring to Florida to days filled with sunshine and golf and the other has dreams about buying a RV and driving across the country.

In either event, the dreams of both spouses need to be accounted for in the financial plan. The only way that can happen is if both partners communicate their hopes and dreams.

Why you need a prenup (and an updated estate plan)

According to a study conducted by the American Academy of Matrimonial Lawyers (AAML), 62% of divorce attorneys in a survey reported an increase in the number of clients requesting prenuptial agreements in recent years. Among those who reported an increase, 51% said it was Millennials who were driving the increase – probably because they were putting off marriage and children until later to benefit their careers, so they were entering marriage with more assets (and more debt).

A prenuptial agreement is a written contract agreed to by both partners before a marriage outlines the assets of each and what will happen to those assets during the marriage and in event of a divorce.

Almost 50 percent of marriages in the U.S. end in divorce or separation.

Sixty percent of second marriages end in divorce and 73 percent of third marriages. Marriages are also much more complicated today, between second and third unions and blended families. I have one friend who still fumes over the fact that his brother, a high-ranking corporate executive, never got around to updating his estate plan after he re-remarried. When he died the estate went entirely to his second wife. She refused to share any of his multi-million-dollar estate with his children from the previous marriage.

There are also countless stories of people passing away and forgetting to update their beneficiaries on their investment accounts, life insurance and other assets. One veteran financial planner told the story of a man who never got around to changing his beneficiary designation to his wife when he married. When he died young and unexpectedly, the very large insurance proceeds went instead to his mother, who was wealthy. She disliked his widow, so she refused to share the proceeds even though she didn't need the money.

Sometimes one partner objects, but many attorneys and financial experts strongly recommend a pre-nuptial. Financial guru and author Suze Orman is among them. "I get too many emails from older women and men telling me that they've just lost everything because of a divorce," she told CNBC in an interview.

In these days when people get married later in life, they also go into marriage with loads of student debt or assets. A prenup can protect one partner from the other's debt. But it can also commit each partner to complete financial transparency going into a marriage and protect assets you want to keep in the family.

If there is no prenup, in the event of divorce, the laws of your state will apply. And those vary greatly.

Divorce late in life can devastate your retirement

Baby Boomers are divorcing at an unprecedented rate. Divorce among people over 50 is so prevalent today it has its own moniker: "gray divorce."

Also divorce rates are not the same among demographics. According to one survey 42 percent of Black Americans had been divorced or married more than once. The rate for White Americans was 38 percent for men and 36 percent for women.

One in four Americans going through divorce is over 50. A Pew Research Center study found that the divorce rate for people over 50 has doubled since 1990.[70]

There are a multitude of reasons for the trend. People are living longer, and the number of second and third marriages is increasing, and as we said earlier, they have an even higher rate of divorce than first marriages.

It's certainly not good for your retirement finances.

If you are divorced in retirement, your retirement money will be cut in half. That nest egg you worked so hard to accumulate must now be split and support two households instead of one. A pension earned during marriage is usually property of both spouses. If you are married the whole time and had a pension, it is cut in half. If you had an IRA, that is cut in half. This can cause people to work longer and delay retirement, or it can force a change in lifestyle.

Health care is another concern. Often one spouse is on the other's company health care plan. That means that spouse will be forced to find health insurance on the open market, which can be an expensive proposition.

And as I said earlier, usually one spouse handles the finances. That can leave the other spouse, who may not be as financially savvy, totally unprepared to handle their post-divorce finances.

Tips for positive money discussions with your partner or spouse

- **Set a specific date and time for a discussion.** If it's on both of your calendars, it's much more likely to happen.

- **Avoid placing blame.** Even if one spouse is to blame for financial difficulties, avoid making him or her defensive, and instead focus on how you can do better in the future and get your spouse to buy into a plan for the future.
- **Focus on shared goals.** Instead of the differences, try to focus on the goals that you both support, such as a new house in three years or a new car next year.
- **Listen carefully to your partner.** Make sure your partner feels like their input and opinions are part of the plan. They should not feel like they are being told what to do.
- **Do not let this discussion turn into an argument.** By keeping calm during the discussion, you are much more likely to produce a positive outcome.

18

Are reparations part of the solution?

CHAPTER 18

Black Americans have lived under the shadow of state-sanctioned racism for more than 400 years. The brutal institution of slavery was followed by centuries of institutionalized discrimination, violent riots resulting in the massacres of thousands of innocent Black men and women like those in Tulsa, Oklahoma, Rosewood, Fla., New York, Philadelphia, and dozens of other American cities. There were also the lynchings, Jim Crow laws and "sundown towns" which banned Blacks entirely or after dusk.

Then there was mortgage discrimination, unequal education in segregated schools, redlining and housing discrimination, racism and discrimination in hiring and promotions and the killing of unarmed Black men and women by police officers and renegade citizens.

That's why scholars, economists and politicians, both Black and White, have called for reparations to be paid to Black Americans for those generations of suffering and abuse.

"Reparations is a legitimate policy response. And, by the way, when it is a legitimate policy response it has been used by the United States throughout history," says Maya Rockeymoore Cummings, the widow of Rep. Elijah Cummings and CEO of Global Policy Solutions in Washington, D.C. "It just hasn't been used to benefit African Americans. It seems to be used to benefit everybody else. We shouldn't think it is something that is out of bounds for African Americans."

"The American Dream portends that with hard work, a person can own a home, start a business, and grow a nest egg for generations to draw upon. This belief, however, has been defied repeatedly by the United States government's own decrees that denied wealth-building opportunities to Black Americans," says Rashawn Ray and Andrew Perry in a Brookings Institution Report.[71]

William H. Darity, professor of public policy at Duke University and co-author of From Here to Equality: Reparations for Black Americans in the Twenty-First Century, says "Reparations are for the cumulative intergenerational effects of White supremacy."

The average White family has roughly 10 times the amount of wealth as the average Black family and White college graduates have over seven

CHAPTER 18

times more wealth than Black college graduates. Making the American Dream an equitable reality demands the same U.S. government that denied wealth to Blacks restore that deferred wealth through reparations to their descendants in the form of individual cash payments in an amount that will close the Black-White racial wealth divide.[72]

Solutions begin with tackling that huge Black-White wealth gap. Black Americans make up 13% of the nation's population, but their share of the nation's wealth is only 2.5%, Darity said. A report by the Brookings Institution from February says the net worth of a typical White family was $171,000 in 2016, compared to $17,150 for a Black family.[73] It would take trillions to bring Black Americans' share of the nation's wealth to be commensurate with their share of the population, Darity said.

Reparations for Black Americans have been approved in cities and states as diverse as Asheville and Buncombe County, North Carolina, Evanston, Illinois, Providence, RI. The California State Assembly, Durham, North Carolina have approved measures to study reparations. And the House Judiciary Committee voted HR 40, a reparations bill, out of committee in early 2021. That bill was originally introduced by the late Rep. John Conyers (D-Mich.) in 1989. However, reparations are strongly opposed by Senate Republicans.

None of these reparations programs, however, would result in direct monetary awards to the descendants of slaves. Most have suggested yet-to-be determined benefits that might encourage economic growth and business development in the Black community. Other strategies include grants and awards to community social service organizations to combat health disparities and to help fix the years of psychological damage done by racism and discrimination. That begs the question: Are these really reparations. Darity says no.

The National African American Reparations Commission (NAARC) has promoted a 10-point Reparations Program. That program called for:

1. **Apology and Maafa Institute.** A formal apology and creation of an African Maafa (Holocaust) Institute.
2. **Repatriation.** The right of repatriation and creation of an African knowledge program.

3. **Land.** The right to land for social and economic development.
4. **Funds.** Funds for cooperative enterprises and socially responsible economic development.
5. **Health and wellness.** Resources for the health, wellness and healing of Black families and communities.
6. **Education.** Education for community development and empowerment.
7. **Housing and wealth generation.** Affordable housing for healthy Black communities and wealth generation.
8. **Information and communications infrastructure.** Strengthening Black America's information and communications infrastructure.
9. **Sacred sites and monuments.** Preserving Black sacred sites and monuments.
10 **Criminal Justice System.** Repairing the damages of the "criminal injustice system."

Support for Reparations

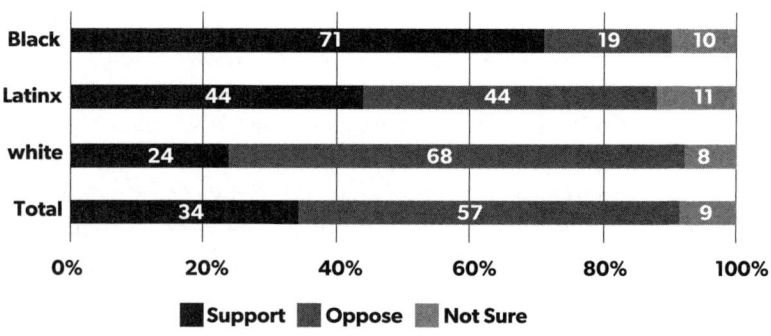

Note: Not all values add to 100 percent because of rounding.

CHAPTER 18

What form should real reparations take?

Options for the actual payment of reparations might include putting funds into individual endowments, offering programs that would increase home ownership among Black citizens, and providing Black people with accounts that will give them direct access to those funds, she said.

Thomas Creamer, professor of public policy at the University of Connecticut, who has been studying reparations for two decades, put the cost of slavery reparations alone—excluding subsequent discrimination or costs of Jim Crow laws—at $18 trillion to $19 trillion, which he called a "conservative estimate."

Darity and Kristen Mullen in their book "From Here to Equality" say the total amount of reparations should be dictated by the amount necessary to eliminate the wealth disparities between Black and White Americans. That would require an expenditure of $10 to $12 trillion, or $200,000 to $250,000 per eligible recipient over 10 years.

They argue that payments should be made directly to eligible recipients, but not necessarily with cash. Assistance could be in the form of trust accounts or endowments that pay out over a period of years. But they also argue that those accounts must be controlled by the recipients, not a third part.

One reason for the trust accounts is that people who come into a huge amount of money, whether it's inheritance or lottery winnings, usually lose it, spend it or end up in bankruptcy. For example, an MIT study found that lottery winners, because of their inexperience with large sums of money, are more likely to file for bankruptcy in three to five years than the average American.[74]

Who would qualify for reparations?

There's a debate even among the leading proponents of reparations. Some say reparations should be limited to those who have direct lineage to slavery. Others say you should look at the effects of slavery, not just the act of slavery. You should consider every way that slavery has shaped

CHAPTER 18

American society, including Jim Crow, unequal education, redlining and even police brutality.

"Reparations do not need to be just limited to the policy of reparations for slavery," says Rockeymoore Cummings. "Remember that there are people in this lifetime who were forced to go to separate and unequal schools because of Jim Crow segregation. That is just as legitimate reason for reparative solutions as the institution of slavery itself."

Darity and Mullen say that there are basically two criteria for eligibility for reparations payments. "An individual would have to demonstrate that one ancestor was enslaved in the United States." Or, they would have to prove that they identified as Black, Negro, or African American at least 12 years before enactment of a reparations project or study commission by making public their response to the race question on the US Census.

In the U.S., private organizations are using their own records to identify eligible recipients.

Georgetown University is raising $400,000 a year to benefit the descendants of 272 enslaved people who were sold to keep the college afloat two centuries ago. Princeton Theological Seminary implemented a $28 million plan that includes scholarships to descendants of enslaved Africans. Brown University is considered by many the model for programs like these. It released a report in 2006 on its founders' connection to slavery and created a center to research slavery and injustice.

Mary Frances Berry, attorney, historian, and former chair of the US Civil Rights Commission, wrote a book on Callie House, a former slave who started a nationwide movement for slavery reparations in the early 1900s, My Face Is Black Is True: Callie House and the Struggle for Ex-Slave Reparations. House, a mother of five, formed a nationwide organization with chapters and members who paid 25 cents a year. They met in churches and petitioned the US courts for reparations. The U.S. government eventually shut down the movement by charging House with mail fraud and sending her to prison in 1917. "My own position is that if there are ever reparations, they should give them first to the people whose names are on those petitions," Berry said. "Those people took great risks."

19

Fixing the wealth gap: Some real strategies

CHAPTER 19

Programs and policies for closing the racial wealth gap

What could be done to help close America's racial wealth gap? Economists, social scientists and activists have offered a variety of suggestions:

Baby Bonds

The federal government could create what is being called Baby Bonds. The idea was proposed in a report by economist William H. Darity and Darrick Hamilton of Ohio State University. A similar plan has been proposed by Ric Edelman, a nationally recognized personal finance expert and author and founder of Edelman Financial Engines. The plans would call for the government to give every child born in the United States a savings account at birth. The Darity/Hamilton plan calls for $1,000 while Edelman proposes $7,500.

Sen. Cory Booker (D-N.J.) has sponsored baby bonds legislation modeled after the Darity/Hamilton proposal. The U.S. government would put the $1,000 in an interest-bearing account and then contribute up to $2,000 every year until the child turned 18. Lower-income children would receive the largest payments. The money could only be tapped, starting at 18, for things like a down payment on a home, college tuition or other "wealth-building" activities.

According to Booker's office, by age 18, the poorest children would have about $46,200; children of the wealthiest parents would have roughly $1,700.

The Darity/Hamilton proposal would cut America's racial gap by half, according to an analysis by Morningstar, a financial services firm. "We find that baby bonds can have a significant impact on the wealth gap when examining the wealth available to each child when reaching 18."[75]

Edelman's plan, meanwhile, would not depend on the government or taxpayers. Instead, these Baby Bonds would be funded by people buying bonds similar to those issued during World War II. Investors would get their money back, plus interest, when the bonds mature in 20 years.

The idea of Baby Bonds idea is favored by 42% of Americans, according to a Prosperity Now survey — 53% of Blacks and 37% of Whites.

Support for Baby Bonds Programs

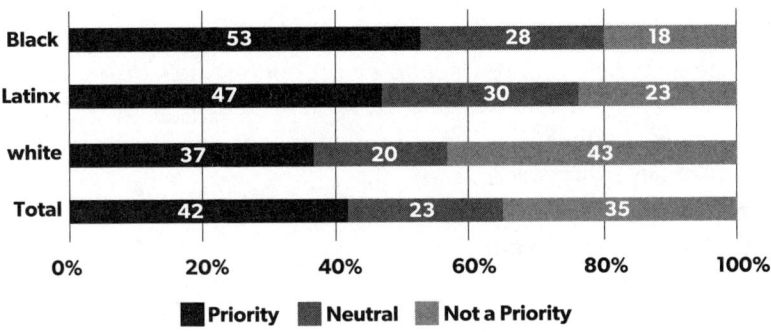

Guaranteed income

Maya Rockeymoore Cummings, CEO of Global Policy Solutions, a Washington-D.C. based policy firm, said some of the most promising strategies to reduce the wealth gap are the strategies that would address poverty through guaranteed income for those whose labor is selectively marginalized in this country. "I think that holds great promise," she said.

Atlanta Councilman Amir Farokhi said in an opinion piece in MarketWatch.com that such a policy answers Rev. Martin Luther King's call for guaranteed income in his last book.

"Piecemeal and pygmy solutions don't suffice," Farokhi wrote. "Guaranteed income offers benefits where other policies have left gaps. At its most fundamental, guaranteed income provides individuals regular cash payments as a means to provide steady footing and improve their well-being. This isn't so different from the COVID-19 stimulus payments that many Americans have received, part of an effort estimated to save 12 million Americans from descending into poverty."[76]

Below-market housing opportunities

Also promising are housing strategies that guarantee below market rate housing opportunities and homeownership opportunities, "not just in terms of homeownership, but in terms of new builds, but re-populating communities where they have been decimated by disinvestment over time in places like Baltimore," Rockeymoore Cummings said.

"These strategies would give people an opportunity to have a piece of the wealth pie through renovation subsidies and other things that can help them to maintain and keep properties in rapidly growing areas where equity is increasing," she said.

End the Black tax on housing

According to research from MIT, Black Americans pay more than White Americans to own a home, which makes it harder for Black Americans to accumulate housing wealth at the same rate as White Americans.

The MIT researchers found that Black Americans pay $743 more in mortgage interest payments, $550 more in mortgage insurance premiums and $390 more a year in property taxes. That amounts to $13,000 over the life of the loan.[77]

The report said those inequities make it impossible for Black households to build housing wealth at the same rate as White households. Elimination of those additional costs would cut in half the $130,000 gap in retirement savings between Black and White families.

The study also found that Black Americans paid higher interest rates due to fewer refinance opportunities, which results in Black homeowners paying "approximately another $475 per year more than White homeowners (a loss of retirement savings of nearly $20,000).

State-sponsored retirement programs

Access to a retirement plan through an employer greatly increases the likelihood that workers will save for retirement. The lack of a retirement plan especially pronounced for workers at small companies and for some racial and ethnic minorities, including Black Americans. According to the

U.S. Bureau of Labor Statistics, 35% of private sector workers—around 43 million Americans—work for firms with fewer than 100 employees.[78] But only 48% of those firms offer retirement plans for their workers, compared with 94% of firms with 500 or more employees.

Nearly three quarters of the states have enacted or proposed legislation for a state-sponsored retirement program. Some have made it mandatory that employers offer the programs, while others have made them voluntary.

Nearly a dozen states have or are slated to have active plans in 2021, including mandatory (requiring employers to participate) ones in Oregon, California and Illinois, Connecticut, Maryland, Maine and New Jersey. New York, Vermont, Washington, Massachusetts and New Mexico have active programs that are voluntary. Colorado and Virginia have passed legislation for mandatory programs but have not announced official start dates.[79]

These state-sponsored plans generally focus on people working for small companies, as well as younger workers, minorities, and low- to moderate-income earners. They are usually designed as Roth IRAs, invest in low-risk investments. Some automatically enroll employees via payroll deduction, but they allow workers an opt out.

Government intervention

In recognition of the 100th anniversary of the Tulsa Massacre, the Biden-Harris Administration announced plans and programs that would narrow the racial wealth gap by expanding access to two of the biggest wealth creators in Black and disadvantaged communities – home ownership and business ownership. Among the proposals:

- Address racial discrimination in the housing market by launching an interagency governmental effort to address inequity in home appraisals and combat housing discrimination.
- Use the federal government's purchasing power to increase federal contracting with small and disadvantaged businesses by 50 percent. That would amount to an additional $100

billion over five years and help more Black Americans become entrepreneurs.
- A new $10 billion Community Revitalization fund.
- A new Neighborhood Homes Tax Credit to attract private investment in the development and rehabilitation of affordable homes for low- and moderate-income homebuyers.
- $31 billion in small business programs to increase access to capital for small businesses and provide technical assistance to socially and economically disadvantaged business owners seeking access to federal contracts.

Pay reparations to Black Americans

Darity estimates the cost of reparations would be $10 to $12 trillion. The cost would include a $200,000 to $250,000 cash transfer to each eligible participant, probably in the form of trust accounts or endowments, he noted.

In a recent Prosperity Now survey, 71% of Black respondents supported reparations payments; 24% of White respondents did.

A host of municipalities and states, including California and Asheville, N.C., have approved reparation resolutions, though none of them call for direct payments to African Americans.

H.R. 40, a bill to create a commission to study reparations to African Americans for slavery, was originally sponsored by U.S. Rep. John Conyers in 1989. It is currently sponsored by U.S. Sheila Jackson Lee.

Corporate Accountability

Following the protests that took place around the world after the killings of George Floyd and Breonna Taylor, a multitude of corporations accounted for new initiatives aimed at improving the business, job and economic opportunities for Black Americans. Some of the most prominent:

PepsiCo announced a five-year, $400 million initiative that includes the goal of increasing Black managerial representation by 30% and more than doubling business with Black-owned suppliers.

CHAPTER 19

Adidas said it would fill 30 percent of its new positions with Black or Hispanic workers.

Bank of America committed to a four-year, $1 billion program to strengthen economic opportunities in communities of color.

PayPal committed $530 million to supporting Black and minority-owned businesses and increasing its commitment to diversity and inclusion within the company.

Comcast dedicated $100 million over three years for diversity and inclusion, including grants and partnerships with civil rights organizations. Increased diversity and inclusion in its hiring and training and more focus on Black creators across its media platforms.

Ben and Jerry's said it would support the fight against systematic racism, including supporting federal legislation advocating slavery reparations.

Sephora said it will devote 15 percent of its shelf space to products produced by Black-owned businesses.

Netflix said it would put 2 percent of its cash into financial institutions and organizations to "directly support Black communities in the U.S." That would include $25 million invested in Black financial institutions serving low-income communities.

Google vowed that minorities would represent 30 percent of its executive staff by 2025.

Andreessen Horowitz, an investment firm, donated $2.2 million to start a program designed to support entrepreneurs from underserved communities. The company will provide entrepreneurs with seed capital and training to help start their businesses.

Apple said it will create an entrepreneurship camp for Black software developers to promote their best work and ideas and increase the number of Black-owned.

Estee Lauder said it would increase the percentage of Black employees at all levels in the company so that they would mirror the percentage of Black Americans in the U.S. population within the next five years. It also said it would double recruits from historically Black colleges and universities in the next two years and it would increase supplies purchased from Black-owned businesses.

Facebook pledged to double the number of its Black and Hispanic employees by 2023 and increase the number of Blacks in leadership positions by 30 percent over the next five years. It also committed to spend at least $100 million annually with Black-owned suppliers.

PayPal created a $500 million fund to support Black and minority businesses by strengthening ties with community banks and credit unions serving underrepresented communities. It also said it would invest directly in Black and other minority start-ups. An additional $10 million was committed for grants to assist Black-owned businesses affected by Covid-19.

PepsiCo said it would increase its number of Black managers by 30 percent by 2025 and committed to adding more than 250 Black employees to management positions, including a minimum of 100 Black employees to the executive ranks. The company said it would double spending with Black-owned suppliers and create more jobs for Blacks at its marketing agencies.

SoftBank said it would start a $100 million fund to invest in companies led by minority entrepreneurs in the United States.

Index

A
AARP, 46, 47, 90, 184
Abrams, Nicholas, 16, 29, 56, 100, 150–151, 158, 178
Acorns, 54, 180
Adidas, 175
Affordable Care Act, 101, 103–104
African Americans. *See* Black individuals and households; Black-White wealth gap; *specific topics*
agricultural workers
    Black, decline since 1910 of, 18
    Social Security Act and, 8, 19
AJW Financial Partners, 16, 56, 100, 150–151, 158, 178
Allianz Life survey, 25, 26, 32
Andreessen Horowitz (investment firm), 175
annuities
    for Blacks compared with Whites, benefits of, 68
    caution with, 66–67
    with FERS, 65
    joint survivor, 68–69
    pension and, 66, 68–69
    single life, 68
    types and benefits of, 67–68, 69
Apple, 93, 175
apps
    for budgeting, 54
    financial literacy, 116, 179
Ariel Academy, 111–112
assisted living costs, 107–108
Association of African American Financial Advisors, 37, 178
athletes, Black, 90, 116, 179
automobile
    expenses, 51, 52–53
    insurance, 45, 47, 100–101
    loans, 86–87
    warranties, extended, 52–53

B
Baby Bonds, 170–171
Bailey, Eric, 26, 28, 35, 37, 62, 178

Bank of America, 175
Bankrate.com, 50, 53, 72, 102, 145
banks
    business loan inequities for Blacks, 148, 149, 150
    financial advisors from, 37
    housing loans/appraisal discrimination by, 19–20, 27, 172
Barnes, Harrison, 116, 179
Ben and Jerry's, 175
Berry, Mary Frances, 168
Black Enterprise, 90, 180
Black farmers, 18–19
Black history
    education, 7, 13
    of racism and discrimination, overview, 12, 13, 15–23, 186
Black individuals and households. *See also specific topics*
    consumer data and trends for, 41–42
    COVID-19 disproportionate impact on, 9, 21, 23, 27
    financial management opportunities for, 8–9
    financial management teaching lack for, 11–12
    land historically taken from, 16–17
    public policies historically excluding, 8
    Social Security Act and, 8, 19
    sundown towns bans on, 15, 164
    wealth stripped from, 12, 16–17
Black-White wealth gap
    Baby Bonds solution for, 170–171
    budgeting/budget creation role in, 41
    corporate accountability around, 174–176
    credit scores and, 46, 83
    educational system discrimination role in, 21
    education level relation to, 164–165
    estate planning and, 15, 90
    generational wealth relation to, 26, 28–29
    government intervention in, 173–174
    guaranteed income and, 171
    homeownership disparities role in, 172
    increase over time, 7–8, 9
    inter-related issues behind persistent, 25–26
    long-standing discrimination impacts on, 21, 119, 120
    personal financial behaviors blame for, 7
    programs and policies for closing, 170–176
    progress and predictions around, 12
    public policy drivers for, 8
    reparations and, 165, 174

retirement programs and, state-sponsored, 172–173
single older women illustration of, 15
slavery legacy and labor relation to, 8, 15
solutions for closing, 26–27, 30–31
statistics and data, 7–8, 25, 26, 41, 56, 164–165
at time of death, 15
Black women
    as caregivers, 123
    entrepreneurship/business owners, 114, 125–126, 148–149, 150, 153
    financial well-being and confidence tips for, 124–126
    health disparities for, 119, 123
    income and wealth inequities for, 15, 28, 119–123
    investment and savings for, 120–122
    median wage for, 120
    Social Security dependence for, 122
Bloomberg Savings and Retirement, 149, 180
Booker, Cory, 170
Books, 186–188
Boomerang kids, 143–144
Brooks, Rodney A. (website resource), 185
Brooks, Sheila, 154
Brown, Tyson, 81, 119
Brown vs. the Board of Education, 20
Bruce, Willa and Charles, 16–17
budgeting/budget creation
    apps for, 54
    asset building role in, 42
    avoidance reasons, 41
    Black-White wealth gap and, 41
    for Black women financial well-being, 124
    cable, cell phone, and internet in, 46
    credit card debt, 47
    for emergency fund, 49
    expenses cutting areas and tips for, 44–47
    family sacrifices and, 145–146
    health insurance considerations in, 104
    insurance options considerations and, 44–45, 104
    monthly differences and awareness in, 46
    mortgages and, 45–46
    retirement readiness relation to, 42, 137
    statistics on, 41
    steps in, 43–44
    stress and, 41

business development and ownership, 9, 100
    Black, challenges with, 28, 148–150, 152, 153, 154, 155
    for Black women, 114, 125–126, 148–149, 150, 153
    book on, 187
    business plan for, 151–152
    capacity lack and, 155
    COVID-19 and Black, 23, 149
    education ongoing in successful, 153
    failure rate around, 28, 148–149, 150
    financial advisors help in, 150–151
    friends and family staff caution in, 154
    loan/lender disparities for Black, 148, 149, 150
    market research importance in, 152
    mentors help for, 154
    organizations and online support for, 155, 177, 180
    retirement savings caution with, 150–151
    survival strategies, 149–155
    venture capitalists and, 150

C

car expenses. *See* automobile
celebrities, Black, 29, 90, 116
Center for Retirement Research, 26, 32
Certified Financial Planner® (CFP), 33, 34, 37
CFA. *See* Chartered Financial Analyst
CFP. *See* Certified Financial Planner
Chartered Financial Analyst (CFA), 33
Chartered Financial Consultant (ChFC), 34
Chartered Life Underwriter (CLU), 34
ChFC. *See* Chartered Financial Consultant
children
    boomerang, 143–144
    financial literacy taught to, 11–12, 113–116, 179
    with special needs in estate planning, 96–97
    supporting adult, 142–145
    tuition for, retirement readiness impacted by, 141–142
Civil Rights Congress, 17–18
Civil Service Retirement System (CSRS), 64–65
Clark.com, 180
CLU. *See* Chartered Life Underwriter
CNBC Personal Finance, 32–33, 160, 180
CNN Business, 181
Comcast, 175

conservatives
    on critical race theory education, 7
    on reparations, 165
Consumer Reports, 101, 181
Consumer spending
    Black, data and trends on, 41–42
    book on reducing, 188
Cook, Lisa D., 83
corporate accountability, 174–176
COVID-19 pandemic
    Black businesses impacted in, 23, 149
    homeownership for Blacks during, 27
    people of color disproportionate impacts from, 9, 21, 23, 27
    retirement savings and, 129–130
    stimulus checks, 171
    unemployment during, 23, 104, 149
    women impacted by, 122–123
Crawford, Anthony, 16
Creamer, Thomas, 167
credit card debt
    book on reducing, 188
    budgeting/budget creation and, 47
    dangers of, 137
    emergencies and, 49
    fixing bad credit score relation to, 86
credit scores
    auto loans and, 86–87
    Black-White wealth gap relation to, 46, 83
    calculation and scale of, 84–85
    co-signing on loan impacts on, 146
    fixing bad, 88
    payday lenders caution around, 87
    racism and discrimination role in Blacks, 83–84
    student loan debt impact on, 85–86
critical race theory, 7
CSRS. See Civil Service Retirement System

D

Daniels, Theodore, 42, 84, 86–87, 113, 115, 117
Darity, William, 15, 26, 164–165, 167, 170, 186
Davis, LeCount, 37
death. *See also* estate planning; life expectancy; life insurance
    Black-White wealth gap at time of, 15
    police violence-related, 28, 174

Depression, Great, 18, 22
disabilities, people with, 96–97, 178
disability insurance, 108–109
discrimination. *See* housing discrimination; racism and discrimination
divorce, 159–161
domestic labor, 8, 19
Douglass, Margaret Crittenden, 20
DuBois, W. E. B., 18

E
Edelman, Ric, 170
education
    Black history, 7, 13
    Black-White wealth gap relation to level of, 164–165
    business ownership, ongoing, 153
    financial literacy, formal, 30, 111–112, 116
educational system discrimination, 20–21
education/tuition investment
    Black students amount of, 141
    for descendants of slaves, 168
    529 plans for, 64, 115, 142
    options for funding, 142–143
    retirement funds used for, 141–142
emergency fund
    benefits of, 49
    for Black women financial well-being, 124–125
    car expenses and, 51
    home warranties and, 53
    household repairs, 51–52
    medical emergencies and, 50–51
    saving for, 49, 53–54
    set-up and access to, 51
    statistics on lack of, 49, 50
    women and, 50
entrepreneurship. See business development and ownership
estate planning
    asset inventory for, 93
    beneficiary designation in, 96, 160
    Black-White wealth gap around, 15, 90
    children with special needs consideration in, 96–97
    for disabilities, people with, 96–97, 178
    dying without a will and, 29, 90, 91
    estate attorneys for, hiring, 91–92
    healthcare directives and, 97–98

    lack of, 15, 26, 29, 90
    marriage and divorce updates in, 159–160
    online accounts and passwords consideration in, 93
    pet care and, 97
    probate and, 90, 91, 94
    taxes and, 92, 94
    top benefits of, 94–95
    will compared with trust in, 95
Estee Lauder, 175–176
exchange traded funds (ETFs), 60, 61, 184

F

Facebook, 176
family sacrifices, financial
    adult children support and, 143–145
    college tuition considerations with, 141–143
    communication clarity importance around, 143–144, 145, 146
    loans and co-signing considerations around, 145, 146
    retirement depletion with, 140–145
Farokhi, Amir, 171
Federal Employee Retirement System (FERS), 65
Fidelity, 62, 71–72, 184
financial advisors/planners
    annuities discussion with, 67–68
    from banks, 37
    Blacks underrepresented as, 30, 37
    Black trust factors with, 35
    Black women financial well-being and, 125–126
    business ownership help from, 150–151
    Certified Financial Planner®, 33, 34, 37
    fee-only compared with asset-based, 39
    fiduciary duty and rules for, 34, 38–39
    finding, tips for, 37–39
    hiring, timing for, 34–35
    insecurities around, 121–122, 125
    interviewing, 38–39
    investment risk assessment by, 60
    marriage financial discussions and, 158–159
    percentage of Americans using, 32–33
    resources and websites, 178–179
    for retirement readiness, 31–35, 72
    Social Security help from, 35
    types of and differences between, 33–34

financial crisis
- book on surviving, 188
- impact for Blacks and, 9, 18, 22–23, 27, 149

financial literacy
- adult, statistics on, 112
- apps, 116, 179
- for Blacks compared with Whites, 112–113
- Black-White wealth gap relation to, 7, 8–9, 112, 117
- Black women need for, 124
- education, formal, 30, 111–112, 116
- generational wealth relation to, 116
- history of racism role in lack of, 13
- parents teaching children about, 11–12, 113–116, 179
- reparations and, 167
- resources and websites for, 179
- school debt and, 116–117
- for women, book on, 187
- for women compared with men, 124

Financial Planning Association, 37, 179

529 plans, 64, 115, 142

Floyd, George, 28, 174

Forbes Personal Finance, 181

"forty acres and a mule," 16

401k
- balance by age, averages, 71, 131
- beneficiary designation on, 96
- Black compared with White participation in, 61
- for Black women financial well-being, 125
- business beginnings with funds from, 150, 151
- "catch-up" contributions for older employees, 32
- characteristics of people maximizing benefits from, 71–72
- contribution by age, averages, 131
- contributions, when to increase, 137–138
- contributions, when to start, 35
- early retirement caution around, 34
- emergencies and, 49
- employer match, exceeding, 73
- employer matching, about, 35, 62
- millionaire, power and danger of, 71–75
- pensions replaced with, 61, 128–129
- resources and sites for investing in, 184
- rolling over, when leaving job, 75
- Roth, 62–63
- taxes and, 31, 62, 75
- wealth building opportunities with, 11, 42

403(b) plans, 63, 96, 121, 122, 129, 133

457 plans, 63
Freedmen's Bureau, 16
From Here to Equality (Darity and Mullen), 15, 164, 167, 186

G

generational wealth. See also estate planning
    Black-White wealth gap relation to, 26, 28–29
    financial literacy relation to, 116
    institutionalized racism impacting, 12
    investing retirement funds for, 74
    life insurance lack and, 29
    life insurance views of Blacks for, 100
    race violence impact on, 16
    solutions for, 31
    statistics on, 116
genocide, 17–18
Get What's Yours (Kotlikoff, Moeller, and Solman), 186
Get What's Yours for Health Care (Moeller), 186
Get What's Yours for Medicare (Moeller), 187
GI Bill, 19
Goalsetter, 116, 179
Godfrey, Neale, 123
Goldman Sachs, 57, 153
Google, 175
government employees, 31, 61, 63, 64–65, 68
Great Depression, 18, 22
Great Recession (2008-2009), 9, 22–23, 27, 149
Greenberg, Cheryl Lyn, 18

H

Hamilton, Darrick, 26
Hannon, Kerry, 181, 187
health and wellness. See also COVID-19 pandemic; life expectancy
    Black women disparities around, 119, 123
    estate planning and directives around, 97–98
    housing discrimination impact for, 19
    inequities for Blacks, 22, 77, 123
    medical emergency fund and, 50–51
    working past retirement impact on, 133
healthcare system
    access and health inequities for Blacks, 22
    books on, 186
    racism and discrimination in, 21–22
health insurance. See also Medicare

Affordable Care Act, 101, 103–104
    Black-White disparities around, 101
    books on, 186–187
    costs, obstacles around, 104
    divorce impact on, 161
    long-term care, 107–108
    statistics, 103
    types and factors, 103–109
Health Savings Account (HSA), 65–66, 105
Hilton, Ebony Jade, 77, 119, 123
homeownership
    Black compared with White, statistics, 25, 27, 28, 45, 46, 56, 83, 172
    Black-White wealth gap relation to, 172
    COVID-19 impact for Black, 27
    home warranties importance in, 53
    insurance, 47
    mortgage disparities with, 30, 45–46
    property tax burden inequities and, 29–30, 45–46
    renters net worth compared with, 56
    reverse mortgages and, 134–136
    wealth creation through, 31, 42, 172
Homestead Act, 8
House, Callie, 168
household repairs, 51–52
housing discrimination
    Black military veterans and, 19
    Great Recession and, 27
    Homestead Act in history of, 8
    loans/lenders and, 19–20, 27, 172
    with redlining practice by banks, 19–20
    strategies for reducing, 172
HSA. See Health Savings Account

I

income disparities, 171. See also Black-White wealth gap
    for Black women, 15, 28, 119–123
    GI Bill and, 19
    Social Security disparities relation to, 77, 81
    statistics, 25, 26, 56
Individual Retirement Account (IRA)
    beneficiary designation on, 96
    contributions and penalties with, 63
    emergencies and, 49
    401k rolled over into, 75

Roth, 63, 173
  setting up, 138
  taxes and, 63, 94
insurance. See also health insurance; life insurance
  broker, tips for finding, 109
  budgeting and, 44–45, 104
  disability, 108–109
  racism and discrimination historically around, 100–101
investing and saving. See also annuities; retirement readiness and plans; stock market investments
  automated, 137–138, 180
  Black women income inequities impacts on, 120–122
  books on, 187
  compound interest and, 57–58
  data and trends for Blacks, 56
  for emergency fund, 49, 53–54
  ETFs and, 60, 61, 184
  529 plans for education, 64, 115, 142
  for generational wealth, 74
  government employees, 31, 61, 63, 64–65, 68
  HSAs for healthcare, 65–66, 105
  mutual funds, 60, 62, 64, 67, 121, 125, 184
  "Rule of 72" for doubling money in 7 years, 59
  tips for increasing, 130–138
  TSP, 65
  25-year return example for, 57–58
  working after 65 impacts for, 133
Investing for Dummies (Tyson), 187
Investopedia.com, 181
IRA. See Individual Retirement Account

J
Jim Crow laws, 15, 21–22, 29, 120, 164, 167–168
Johnson, Andrew, 16

K
Kelly, Dawn, 114, 125–126, 148–149, 150, 153
Kiplinger's Personal Finance News, 182
Kotlikoff, Laurence, 186
Krantz, Matthew, 187

L
labor laws and policies, 8
land grants and ownership, 8, 16–17. See also homeownership

life expectancy
- annuities considerations of, 66, 68
- for Blacks compared with Whites, 81
- COVID-19 and people of color, 9
- retirement savings and, 132, 133
- Social Security considerations with, 79, 81
- statistics, 79

life insurance
- Black families lack of, 29
- Black families views on, 100
- types and factors, 101–103

Lincoln, Abraham, 16
literacy, 12. See also financial literacy
loans/lenders
- automobile, 86–87
- business, inequities for Blacks, 148, 149, 150
- family sacrifices and caution around, 145, 146
- housing discrimination around, 19–20, 27, 172
- payday, 47, 49, 87, 116
- student debt and, 85–86, 116–117, 142, 144
- venture capitalists, 150

M

Malveaux, Julianne, 16
marriage
- divorce rates for, 159–160, 161
- estate planning and, 159–160
- financial advisors help in, 158–159
- financial communications in, 158–159, 161–162
- financial stress on, 157–158
- prenuptial agreements in, 159–160
- wealth boost for Whites compared with Blacks, 8

Martin, Roland, 23, 149, 155
massacres and riots, 15, 16, 17f, 164, 173
McNair, Yvonne, 121, 125, 151, 153, 154
medical emergencies, 50–51
Medicare
- book on, 187
- coverage and premiums, 105–107
- hospital discrimination and, 22
- HSA alternative for, 65
- website resources for retirement, 184

military veterans, Black, 19
Millennials, 38, 41, 130, 137, 143, 159

Mint.com, 41, 54
Moeller, Philip, 186–187
Money.com, 182
Moriaf, Ken, 80
mortgages
    racial disparities with, 30, 45–46
    reverse, for boosting retirement savings, 134–136
Motley Fool, 51, 182
Mullen, A. Kirsten, 15, 164, 167–168, 186
mutual funds, 60, 62, 64, 67, 121, 125, 184
My Face Is Black Is True (Berry), 168

N
National African American Reparations Commission (NAARC), 165–166
National Minority Supplier Development Council (NMSDC), 155, 177
Netflix, 175
Never Too Old to Get Rich (Hannon), 187
Next Avenue, 185
NMSDC. See National Minority Supplier Development Council
Nourse, Rene, 25, 28
nursing home costs, 107–108

O
Obama Administration, 39, 83, 111
Obamacare, 101, 103–104
Online Investing for Dummies (Krantz), 187
online resources, 81, 177–185
Orman, Suze, 160
Owens, Deborah, 179, 187

P
Partridge, Charlie, 150, 152, 153
Paul, Chris, 116, 179
payday loans/lenders, 47, 49, 87, 116
PayPal, 175, 176
pensions, 61, 66, 68–69, 128–129
people of color. See also Black individuals and households; Black-White wealth gap; specific topics
    COVID-19 disproportionate impacts on, 9, 21, 23, 27
    educational system racism impact for, 20–21
    retirement readiness risk for, 25, 26, 32
PepsiCo, 174, 176
Perry, Andrew, 164
personal finance sites, 179–183

police violence, 15, 18, 28, 174
prenuptial agreement, 159–160
property taxes, 29–30, 45–46
A Purse of Your Own (Owens), 187

Q
Quakers, 20, 21

R
racism and discrimination. See also housing discrimination
    auto insurance and, 45
    Black psyche and culture impacted by, 56
    Black-White wealth gap relation to long-standing, 21, 119, 120
    book on history and cost of, 186
    corporate accountability around, 174–176
    credit scores relation to, 83–84
    domino effect with, 23
    educational system, 20–21
    in healthcare system, 21–22
    history of, 12, 13, 15–23, 186
    institutionalized, 12, 15, 20–21, 164
    insurance relation to history of, 100–101
    reparations for, 164–168, 174, 186
    state-sanctioned, 12, 15, 17–19
    understanding history of, importance of, 13
Ramsey, Dave, 52–53, 114, 179
Ray, Rashawn, 164
real estate. See homeownership; housing discrimination; land grants and ownership
recessions. See financial crisis
reparations
    book on, 186
    cost of, estimates, 167, 174
    forms of, 167
    NAARC program on, 165–166
    qualification for, 167–168
    slavery and, 164, 167–168
    support for, 165, 166, 168, 174
resource guide and websites, 177–185
retirement readiness and plans. See also annuities; 401k; Social Security; Individual Retirement Account
    account types and considerations for, 61–69
    age discrimination and loss of work impacting, 134
    age legally for full retirement relation to, 78

    amount of savings needed for, 128–129
    Black-White gap in, 25, 31, 32, 41, 61, 77, 121
    budgeting and, 42, 137
    business start-up funding and, 150–151
    characteristics of people with excellent, 71–72
    COVID-19 pandemic and, 129–130
    CSRS, 64–65
    divorce and, 160–161
    downsizing and cutting expenses for, 136–137
    early retirement caution and, 34
    family sacrifices impacting, 140–145
    FERS, 65
    financial planners importance for, 31–35, 72
    4 percent rule for, 69
    403(b) plans and, 63, 96, 121, 122, 129, 133
    457 plans and, 63
    inability to retire due to inadequate, 128–138
    life expectancy and, 132, 133
    median amount saved for, 71
    mistakes with, 11, 31–32
    mortgage/property tax inequities impact on, 30, 45–46
    obstacles to, 129–130
    overspending caution with, 74
    pensions, decline in, 61
    for people of color, risk around, 25, 26, 32
    required minimum distributions with, 64
    resources and sites for, 184–185
    reverse mortgages and, 134–136
    savings boost tips, 137–138
    Social Security dependence role in, 25–26
    state-sponsored, 172–173
    stock market investments role for, 25, 72, 74
    strategies for lifetime income with, 68–69
    taxes considerations for security of, 75
    tuition for children impact on, 141–142
    working past 65 and, 130–134
riots and massacres, 15, 16, 17f, 164, 173
Robeson, Paul, 18
Rockeymoore Cummings, Maya, 7–9
    on financial literacy role in wealth disparities, 117
    on guaranteed income, 171
    on housing strategies, 172
    on racial and gender wage disparity, 119–120, 126
    on reparations for slavery and racism, 16, 164, 168
    on slavery labor and wealth for White families, 15
Rogers, John, 111

S

saving. See investing and saving; retirement readiness and plans
SBA. See Small Business Administration
SCORE (Service Corps of Retired Executives), 155, 177
segregation
    in education, 20
    in healthcare system, 21–22
    Jim Crow laws and, 15, 21–22, 29, 120, 164, 167–168
Senior Planet, 185
Sephora, 175
Service Corps of Retired Executives (SCORE), 155, 177
SFE&PD. See Society for Financial Education and Professional Development
Singletary, Michelle, 182, 188
slavery
    "forty acres and a mule" policy after, 16
    reparations and, 164, 167–168
    state-sanctioned racism history beginnings with, 12, 15
    White wealth from, 8, 15
Small Business Administration (SBA), 155, 177
Social Security
    benefit factors and calculations, 78–79, 80
    Black agricultural and domestic labor excluded from, 8, 19
    books on, 186
    delaying or taking, factors in, 79–80
    dependence on, for Blacks, 77, 80, 122
    dependence on, risk with, 25–26, 32, 78
    disparities around, 25–26, 77–78, 80, 122
    financial planner help with, 35
    full retirement age relation to, 78
    online resource for checking, 81, 185
    taking early, caution with, 132
    for women compared with men, 120
Social Security Administration website, 81, 185
Society for Financial Education and Professional Development (SFE&PD), 42, 84, 113, 179
SoftBank, 176
Solman, Paul, 186
Special Needs Alliance, 96–97, 178
Stanton, Cecilia, 26
stock market investments
    age considerations with, 60
    for Blacks compared with Whites, 25, 28, 121
    Black trust and risk factors in, 28, 59

generational wealth and, 74
individual stock investment with, 60
retirement readiness and, 25, 72, 74
returns over time for, 57
risk considerations with, 59–60
student loan debt, 85–86, 116–117, 142, 144
sundown towns, 15, 164

T
taxes
- estate planning and, 92, 94
- 401k and, 31, 62, 75
- 403(b) plans and, 63
- HSA and, 65
- IRA and, 63, 94
- property, inequities around, 29–30, 45–46
- retirement readiness consideration of, 75

Taylor, Breonna, 174
Thrift Savings Plan (TSP), 65
Transamerica Center for Retirement Studies, 128, 130
trusts. See estate planning
TSP. See Thrift Savings Plan
tuition. See education/tuition investment
Tulsa Massacre, 15, 16, 164, 173
The 21-Day Financial Fast (Singletary), 188
Tyson, Eric, 187

U
unemployment
- for Blacks during financial crisis, 18, 22–23, 149
- during COVID-19 pandemic, 23, 104, 149
- emergency fund and, 50

United Nations Genocide Convention, 17–18
Urban Institute, 28, 83, 103
Urban Wealth Management, 25
USA TODAY, 136, 182
U.S. News and World Report, 183

V
Van Court, Tanya, 116
Vanguard, 62, 71, 138, 183, 184
Venable, Abraham, 153
venture capitalists, 150

W

Walker, Antoine, 116
Wallethub.com, 47, 183
Wall Street Journal personal finance, 183
Washington Post personal finance, 183
websites, 81, 177–185
What to Do with Your Money When Crisis Hits (Singletary), 188
White individuals and households (compared with Blacks). See also Black-White wealth gap
- annuities for, 68
- critical race theory education impact for, 7
- financial crisis and unemployment for, 22–23
- financial literacy for, 112–113
- health insurance for, 101
- homeownership for, 25, 27, 28, 45, 46, 56, 83, 172
- life expectancy for, 81
- marriage impact on wealth for, 8
- post-slavery land grants for, 16
- retirement readiness and plans for, 25, 31, 32, 41, 61, 77, 121
- single older women wealth for, 15
- stock market investments for, 25, 28, 121

widowhood, 93, 96, 129–130, 136, 158
wills. See estate planning
women. See also Black women
- book on financial literacy for, 187
- as caregivers, 123
- COVID-19 pandemic impacts for, 122–123
- emergency fund likelihood for, 50
- financial literacy for men compared with, 124
- income and wealth inequities for, 15, 28, 119–123
- Social Security for men compared with, 120

World War II veterans, 19

Financial planning resource guide

ENTREPRENEUR SUPPORT SITES

U.S. Small Business Administration (SBA) Small Business Development Centers
www.SBA.gov

These Centers provide management assistance to current and potential small business owners by offering expertise provided by people recruited from professional and trade associations, the legal and baking communities, colleges and universities, chambers of commerce and the Service Corps of Retired Executives (SCORE).

SCORE (Service Corps of Retired Executives)
www.score.org

Score fosters business development through mentoring and education. The mentors are generally successful business owners and corporate executives who volunteer their time and expertise and have tools and resources that are specially geared toward women entrepreneurs. There is also a SCORE for Black Entrepreneurs.

National Minority Supplier Development Council (NMSDC)
www.nmsdc.org

NMSDC matches its 12,000 minority business members with corporations who might purchase their products and services. Its nearly 1,500 corporate members includes many of the nation's largest corporations. The Council has two dozen affiliated regional councils.

ESTATE PLANNING SITES

Special Needs Alliance
www.specialneedsalliance.org

The Special Needs Alliance (SNA) is a national organization comprised of attorneys committed to the practice of disability and public benefits law. Individuals with disabilities, their families and their advisors rely on the SNA to connect them with nearby attorneys who focus their practices on the disability law arena.

FINANCIAL PLANNERS

Association of African American Financial Advisors (QUAD A)
www.aaafainc.com

The Association of African American Financial Advisors (AAAA) serves to expand the community of successful Black financial professionals.

AJW Financial Partners, LLC
www.ajwfinancial.net/Nicolas-Abrams.e282015.htm/

AJW Financial Partners endeavors to know and understand your financial situation and provide you with only the highest quality information, services, and products to help you reach your goals.

Bailey Wealth Advisors
www.baileywealthadvisors.com

Helps clients design exit strategies from their closely held businesses, invest their money, selecting private money managers, facilitating the exercise of stock options, securing life insurance or designing complicated estate plans.

Ramsey Solutions – Dave Ramsey
www.daveramsey.com

Ramsey Solutions mission is to help people crush debt and build a legacy.

Deborah Owens, America's Wealth Coach™
deborahowens.com

Deborah Owens is America's Wealth Coach™ and is on a mission to help women overcome their fear of investing through coaching, accountability, and support.

Financial Planning Association
www.financialplanningassociation.org

The Financial Planning Association® (FPA®) is the primary membership organization for financial planning practitioners.

FINANCIAL LITERACY

SFE&PD.org
www.sfepd.org

Society for Financial Education and Professional Development is a financial literacy and professional development organization that is dedicated to the premise that financial knowledge contributes to a stronger society and better economy.

Goalsetter.co
www.Goalsetter.co

The site, backed by professional athletes like Chris Paul and Harrison Barnes, helps parents teach their children about financial planning with an app that encourages both savings and education.

PERSONAL FINANCE SITES

Acorns.com
www.acorns.com

Acorns is a robo-advisor, also known as an automated investing services or online advisor.

Bankrate.com
www.bankrate.com

Bankrate's product comparison tools, calculators, and educational content helps consumers make smarter financial decisions.

Black Enterprise
www.Blackenterprise.com

BLACK ENTERPRISE is the premier business, investing, and wealth-building resource for African Americans.

Bloomberg Savings and Retirement
www.bloomberg.com/wealth/savings-and-retirement

Bloomberg delivers business and markets news, data, analysis, and video to the world, featuring stories on everything pertaining to wealth.

Clark.com Investing-Retirement
www.clark.com/personal-finance-credit/investing-retirement/

Clark Howard is a leading consumer advocate and money expert, who has been sharing practical advice to help people save more and spend less for more than 30 years.

CNBC Personal Finance
www.cnbc.com/personal-finance/

Find personal finance top news, headlines, and videos from credit cards, mortgages, retirement, savings, taxes, and more from CNBC's Personal Finance.

CNN Business
www.cnn.com/business

CNN Business (formerly CNN Money) is a financial news and information website.

Consumer Reports (CR)
www.consumerreports.org

As a mission-driven, independent, nonprofit member organization, CR empowers and informs consumers, incentivizes corporations to act responsibly, and helps policymakers prioritize the rights and interests of consumers.

Forbes Personal Finance
www.forbes.com/personal-finance/

Forbes is a leading source for reliable news and updated analysis on Personal Finance.

Investopedia.com Personal Finance
www.investopedia.com/personal-finance/

Since Investopedia was launched in 1999, its mission has been to simplify complex financial information and decisions for readers, giving them the confidence to manage every aspect of their financial life.

Kerry Hannon
www.kerryhannon.com
www.forbes.com/sites/kerryhannon/

Kerry Hannon is a leading authority and strategist on career transitions, entrepreneurship, personal finance and retirement.

Kiplinger's Personal Finance News
www.kiplinger.com

Kiplinger's Personal Finance advises its readers on managing their money, covering investing, retirement planning, taxes, insurance, real estate, buying and leasing a car, health care, travel and financing college.

Michelle Singletary
www.michellesingletary.com/home.html
www.washingtonpost.com/people/michelle-singletary/

Michelle Singletary is a personal finance columnist for The Washington Post. Her award-winning column, "The Color of Money," appears twice a week in dozens of newspapers across the country and is syndicated by The Washington Post News Service and Syndicate.

Money.com_Investing
www.money.com/section/investing/

Money provides up-to-date news, educational resources, and tools that will help you create meaningful investments and lasting returns.

Motley Fool
www.fool.com

Motley Fool provides a variety of solutions to improve many areas of your financial life, including your investment portfolio, personal finances, real estate holdings, company, and career.

USA TODAY
www.usatoday.com/money/personal-finance/

Exclusive news on the markets, personal finance and money management tips from the entire USA TODAY network of more than 5,000 journalists across more than 300 digital properties in 46 states.

U.S. News and World Report
www.money.usnews.com/money/personal-finance

The latest business news and financial news on the market and economy. Get financial advice to wisely invest and manage your personal finances to pay for college, retirement, buying a car, and more.

Vanguard.com
www.vanguard.com

Vanguard gives you access to personalized financial advice, high-quality investments, retirement tools and relevant market insights that help you build a future for those you love.

Wall Street Journal personal finance
www.wsj.com/news/types/personal-finance

Latest News, Articles, Biography, and Photos from "Personal Finance" in The Wall Street Journal.

Wallethub.com
www.wallethub.com

WalletHub's performs three primary functions: 1) Customized credit-improvement advice; 2) Personalized savings alerts; and 3) 24/7 wallet surveillance. These features are supplemented by reviews of financial products, professionals and companies, plus free credit scores and full credit reports that are updated on a daily basis.

Washington Post
www.washingtonpost.com/personal-finance/

Make your money work for you. This is your destination for stories about money and its power to transform our lives.

MUTUAL FUND/401(K)/INVESTING

Fidelity.com Retirement Planning
www.fidelity.com/retirement-planning/overview

No matter where you are in your retirement planning, Fidelity's perspective, tools, and guidance can help you feel more confident and prepared for what's ahead.

Vanguard
www.investor.vanguard.com/home

Vanguard is the world's largest provider of mutual funds and the second-largest provider of exchange-traded funds (ETFs). Vanguard offers manages company-sponsored 401(k)s, and offers brokerage services, variable and fixed annuities, education account services, financial planning, asset management, and trust services.

RETIREMENT SITES

AARP® Money Matters
www.aarp.org/money/

Articles on money management, the latest money advice, social security, retirement and financial tips, news and more.

Medicare
www.medicare.gov

A federal government website managed and paid for by the U.S. Centers for Medicare & Medicaid Services. Medicare provides health insurance coverage to individuals who are age 65 and over, under age 65 with certain disabilities, and individuals of all ages with ESRD.

Next Avenue
www.nextavenue.org

News and information for people over 50. Next Avenue is a digital platform launched by PBS that offers original and aggregated journalism aimed at Baby Boomers. Next Avenue is PBS' first venture to begin on the Internet rather than on broadcast television. It was conceived and developed at Twin Cities Public Television in St. Paul, MN.

Rodney A. Brooks
www.rodneyabrooks.com

Rodney A. Brooks writes about retirement and personal finance issues. He has written about retirement for USA TODAY, The Washington Post and U.S. News & World Report. He has also written for Black Enterprise, Jet Magazine, National Geographic and The Undefeated. "My readers tell me that I translate complicated financial advice into terms that anyone can understand...."

Senior Planet
www.seniorplanet.org

Its mission is to help seniors harness the power of technology no matter their socioeconomic circumstances, geography, educational background or age.

Social Security Administration
www.ssa.gov

The website for the U.S. Social Security Administration. Find information on when to sign up, if you qualify and tips, news and information. www.MySocialSecurity.com is the pathway to your personal account, work history whether you receive benefits or not. You can request a replacement Social Security card or manage your benefits.

BOOKS

From Here to Equality: Reparations for Black America in the 21ˢᵗ Century, By William A. Darity and Kristen Mullen. *From Here to Equality*, William Darity Jr. and A. Kirsten Mullen confront these injustices head-on and make the most comprehensive case to date for economic reparations for U.S. descendants of slavery. After opening the book with a stark assessment of the intergenerational effects of White supremacy on Black economic well-being, Darity and Mullen look to both the past and the present to measure the inequalities borne of slavery. Using innovative methods that link monetary values to historical wrongs, they next assess the literal and figurative costs of justice denied in the 155 years since the end of the Civil War. Finally, Darity and Mullen offer a detailed roadmap for an effective reparations program, including a substantial payment to each documented U.S. Black descendant of slavery. Taken individually, any one of the three eras of injustice outlined by Darity and Mullen-- slavery, Jim Crow, and modern-day discrimination--makes a powerful case for Black reparations. Taken collectively, they are impossible to ignore. University of North Carolina Press, 424 pages.

Get What's Yours: The Secrets to Maxing Out your Social Security, by Laurence Kotlikoff, Philip Moeller, and Paul Solman, *Get What's Yours* has proven itself to be the definitive book about how to navigate the forbidding maze of Social Security and emerge with the highest possible benefits. It is an engaging manual of tactics and strategies written by well-known financial commentators that is unobtainable elsewhere. Simon & Shuster, 384 pages.

Get What's Yours for Health Care: How to Get the Best Care at the Right Price, By Philip Moeller. Healthcare expert Philip Moeller has written a reliable, concise guide to healthcare and health insurance basics. He provides tools that patients need before, during, and after they get medical care. He describes the care we need, the care we don't, and how to deal with doctors, hospitals, and other healthcare providers. Simon & Shuster, 368 pages.

Get What's Yours for Medicare: Maximize Your Coverage, Minimize Your Costs, By Philip Moeller, A coauthor of the *New York Times* bestselling guide to Social Security *Get What's Yours* authors an essential companion to explain Medicare, the nation's other major benefit for older Americans. Learn how to maximize your health coverage and save money. Simon & Shuster, 305 pages.

A Purse of Your Own: An Easy Guide to Financial Security, Deborah Owens. Wealth coach Deborah Owens draws from more than twenty years of experience in the financial services industry for a revolutionary and simple approach to investment literacy: Women can take control of their lives and purses by leveraging the feminine powers of intuition, creativity, and empathy to build personal wealth. Touchstone, 290 pages.

Never Too Old to Get Rich: The Entrepreneur's Guide to Starting a Business Mid-Life, Kerry Hannon. When you think of someone launching a start-up, the image of a twenty-something techie probably springs to mind. However, Gen Xers and Baby Boomers are just as likely to start businesses and reinvent themselves later in life. *Never Too Old to Get Rich* is an exciting roadmap for anyone age 50+ looking to be their own boss and launch their dream business. Wiley, 275 pages.

Investing for Dummies, Eric Tyson. Investing for your future is wise and essential. Of course, you want to make solid investment choices and minimize mistakes. This updated, best-selling guide educates you on investing concepts and lingo so you can make the best decisions in all economies and markets. Understanding how to find and make smart investments is a skill that can be learned, and this book by money-pro Eric Tyson will help you by discovering how to weigh risk vs. return, offering tips on choosing stocks and funds, getting started in real estate and small business, and so much more. For Dummies, 464 pages.

Online Investing for Dummies, Matthew Krantz, Online investing has never been easier – or more potentially confusing. Now that every broker or finance site has its own app, data or approach, it can be all too easy to be misled and make a bad decision. Online Investing for Dummies helps you reduce risk and separates the gimmicks from the gold, pointing investors of all experience levels to the pro-times, calculators, databases, useful sites and peer communities that will lead to success. Updated to include information on mobile trading and the influence of social media on the markets, the book also covers the basics – showing you how to figure out how to invest, find data online and pick an online broker. For Dummies, 10th edition, 2019, 432 pages.

What to Do with Your Money When Crisis Hits: A Survival Guide. Michelle Singletary. From pandemics to recessions, bear markets to energy crises, life is full of financial setbacks. The hard truth is that it's not a matter of if there will be another economic downturn, but when. The important question to ask is this: how do you prevent a crisis from turning into a full-blown catastrophe? Houghton Mifflin Harcourt, 175 pages.

The 21-Day Financial Fast: Your Path to Financial Peace and Freedom, In *The 21-Day Financial Fast,* award-winning writer and *The Washington Post* columnist Michelle Singletary proposes a field-tested financial challenge. For twenty-one days, participants will put away their credit cards and buy only the barest essentials, Zondervan, 242 pages.

Acknowledgements

There are so many people that motivated me to finally write the book that I've been talking about for so many years.

There were friends like Kerry Hannon who pushed me for years to write this book and Michael Days, my best friend of 35 years. I was honored to have him be my sounding board and editors for this book.

Then there is my oldest son and namesake, R. Alan Brooks, who has been pushing me to write a book, any book, for the last 20 years, and my youngest, Andre, whose passion for journalism inspires us every day.

There is my aunt, Pastor Marion Brooks, the matriarch of the Brooks family, who recently celebrated her 100th birthday and has inspired me in new ways over the last few years with her stories of life in Florida and Baltimore in the 1940s and 1950s.

And finally, the four generations of Black women who inspire me every day: my late mother, Mattie B. Brooks, who raised me with the love and encouragement that I still feel today; my wife, life partner and daily inspiration, Dr. Sheila Brooks, who's grit, determination and spirit motivate me every day; and my daughter, Tahira and granddaughter, Dylan, who make me want to want to reach and teach new generations of Black Americans about wealth and finance.

Notes

Chapter One

[1] We charge genocide, the 1951 Black Lives Matter campaign, by Susan A. Glenn, University of Washington Mapping American Social Movements Project.

[2] The USDA issued billions in subsidies this year. Black farmers are still waiting for their share. Patrice Gaines, NBC News, Oct. 28, 2020.

[3] Ann Brown, The Moguldom Nation, Feb. 15, 1921.

[4] Imprisoned for teaching Free Blacks, Brown vs. Board at Fifty, A Century of Racial Segregation, 1849-1950, Library of Congress.

[5] History of Institutional Racism in U.S. Public Schools, Matthew Lynch, The Advocate, October 2019.

[6] Separate and Unequal, Brown vs. Board at Fifty, A Century of Racial Segregation, 1849-1950.

[7] Unequal Opportunity: Race and Education, Linda Darling-Hammond, March 1, 1998, Brookings

[8] History of Institutional Racism in the U.S. Public Schools, The Advocate, October 2019

[9] The Black-White Wealth Gap will widen Educational Disparities During the Coronavirus Pandemic, Dania Francis and Christian E. Weller, Center for American Progress, Aug. 12, 2020.

[10] Desegregation: The Hidden Legacy of Medicare, By Steve Sternberg, U.S. News and World Report, July 29, 2015.

[11] Last hired first fired: How the Great Depression affected African Americans, Christopher Klein, History.com

[12] The Great Recession, education, race and home ownership, Christopher Famighetti and Darrick Hamilton, Economic Policy Institute.

Chapter Two

[13] Examining the Black-White wealth gap, Kriston McIntosh, Emily Moss, Ryan Nunn, and Jay Shambaugh, Brooking Institution, Feb. 27, 2020

[14] Trends in Retirement Security by Race/Ethnicity, By Alecia H. Munnell, Wenliang Hou, and Geoffrey Sanzenbacher, Center for Retirement Research at Boston College, November 2018.

[15] The Urban Institute Urban Wire, New data suggest covid-19 is widening housing disparities by race and income, Solomon Greene and Alanna McCargo, June 2, 2020.

[16] The Urban Institute Urban Wire, New data suggest covid-19 is widening housing disparities by race and income, Solomon Greene and Alanna McCargo, June 2, 2020.
[17] Mapping the Black home ownership gap, Alanna McCargo, Sarah Strochak, Feb. 26, 2018
[18] Black Homeowners Pay More Than "Fair Share" in Property Taxes, By Teresa Wiltz, PEW Stateline Article, June 25, 2020.

Chapter Three

[19] 99 percent of Americans don't use a financial advisor. Here's why. Michelle Fox, CNBC, Nov. 11, 2019.

Chapter Four

[20] It's in the bag: Black consumers' path to purchase, Nielsen Insights, September 19, 2019.
[21] The Unequal Costs of Black Home Ownership, Michelle Aronowitz, Law Office of Michelle Aronowitz; Edward L. Golding, MIT Golub Center for Finance and Policy; and Jung Hyun Choi, Urban Institute, October 1, 2020.
[22] The Unequal Costs of Black Home Ownership, Michelle Aronowitz, Law Office of Michelle Aronowitz; Edward L. Goulding, MIT Golub Center for Finance and Policy; and Jung Hyun Choi, Urban Institute, October 1, 2020.

Chapter Five

[23] Carecredit.com, GoodRx.com
[24] Car Repair estimates and auto repair costs, CarBrain.com
[25] Seven expensive home repairs, Maurie Backman, Fool.com, December 22, 2019
[26] Should you get an extended warranty for your car, Consumer Reports, March 2021.
[27] Bankrate.com, Are Home Warranties Worth It? August 2019

Chapter Six

[28] "Are gains in Black home ownership history?" Laurie Goldman, Urban Institute.
[29] This simple formula tells you how long it will take your money to double – while you sit back and relax, Kathleen Elkins, CNBC, December 2020.
[30] What is the value of annuities?" By Gal Wettstein, Alicia H. Munnell, Wenliang Hou, and Nilufer Gok, Center for Retirement Research at Boston College, March 2021.

Chapter Eight

[31] Vanguard.com, How America Saves, 2019

[32] The Social Security Retirement Age, Congressional Research Service, Updated January 2021.

[33] Minorities and Social Security: An Analysis of Racial and Ethnic Differences in the Current Program, Social Security Bulletin, Vol. 62, No. 2

[34] How to calculate the break-even age for Social Security, Ken Moriaf, Kiplinger, April 7, 2020

Chapter Nine

[35] Breaking down the Black-White home ownership gap, Jung Hyun Choi, The Urban Institute, Feb. 21, 2020.

[36] Myelle Lansat, Grow, Aug. 22, 2019.

[37] The Continued Student Loan Crisis for Black borrowers, Ben Miller, Center for American Progress, Dec. 2, 2019.

[38] Mel Hanson, Student Loan Debt by Race, Educationdata.org, Sept. 24, 2020

Chapter Ten

[39] Receiving an inheritance helps White families more than Black families, Janelle Jones, Economic Policy Institute, Economic Snapshot, Feb. 17, 2017.

[40] How much will a lawyer charge you to write a will, Mary Randolph, J.D., Nolo.com.

[41] Is there a life insurance gap? We surveyed Black and White consumers to learn if there are racial differences in how they perceive and buy life insurance. (Spoiler: There are)

Chapter Eleven

[42] Minority neighborhoods pay higher car insurance premiums than White areas with the same risk, By Julia Angwin, Jeff Larsson, Lauren Kirchner and Surya Mattu, Pro Publica.

[43] Finding the rate of return on your whole life policy, Elizabeth Rivelli, Bankrate.com, Sept. 25, 2020

[44] Workers without health insurance: Who are they and how can policy reach them, By Bowen Garrett, Len M. Nichols and Emily K Greenman, The Urban Institute.

Chapter Twelve

[45] Paul Yakoboski, Annamaria Lusardi, Andrea Hasler, Financial literacy, wellness and resilience among African Americans, TIAA Institute, November 2019.

[46] Paul Yakoboski, Annamaria Lusardi, Andrea Hasler, Financial literacy, wellness and resilience among African Americans, TIAA Institute, November 2019.

[47] Judith Scott-Clayton and Jing Li, Black-White disparity in student loan debt more than triples after graduation, Economic Studies and Brookings, Oct. 20, 2016.

[48] Special Report: Women and Investing, Susan Dziubinski, Morningstar, March 3, 2021

[49] Black women and the wage gap, Fact sheet, National Partnership for Women & Families, March 2021.

Chapter Thirteen

[50] Disparities for women and minorities in retirement savings, David C. John, The Brookings Institution, September 2010.

[51] Women are Building More Wealth, But Racial Gaps Persist, Hannah Hassani, the Urban Institute, March 22, 2018.

[52] Alzheimer's disease and healthy aging, African American Adults, The Centers for Disease Control and Prevention.

Chapter Fourteen

[53] Older Americans in the workforce, Lincoln Plews, United Income/Capital One, April 22, 2019

[54] Working later in life can pay off in more than just income, Harvard Health Letter, Harvard Health Publishing, Harvard Medical School, June 2018.

[55] 2019 Retirement Confidence Study, Employee Benefits Research Institute and Greenwald & Associates, April 23, 2019.

[56] Reverse Mortgages, The Federal Trade Commission Consumer Information, https://www.consumer.ftc.gov/articles/0192-reverse-mortgages

[57] Seniors were sold a risk-free retirement with reverse mortgages. Now the face foreclosure: Urban African American neighborhoods are hardest hit as nearly 100,000 loans have failed, Nick Penzenstadler, Jeff Kelly Lowenstein, USA TODAY, Dec. 18, 2019.

[58] College Debt in America: The Case for Tuition and Loan Repayment Benefits, Guardian's 6th Annual Workplace Benefits Study (2018).

[59] 2019 Parents, Kids and Money Survey, T. Rowe Price survey of 1,005 parents of children aged 8 to 14.

Chapter Fifteen

[60] Fewer Resources, More Debt: Loan debt burdens students at Historically Black Colleges and Universities, United Negro College Fund (UNCF.org)

[61] Trends in Student Aid 2020, The College Board.

[62] Boomerang Generation, Returning to the Nest, TD Ameritrade, May 2019

[63] Leaving the Nest, The Reality About Moving Back in With Parents, Porch.com, survey of 1,001 people about family members, moving in and living situations.

[64] Poll: Many parents have helped adult children financially since 2020, by Barri Segal, Creditcards.com, May 5, 2021.

[65] Survey: Lending cash to loved ones ends badly for nearly half of Americans, Kendall Little, Bankrate.com, September 26, 2019.

Chapter Sixteen

[66] 20 Black-owned business statistics for 2021, Nick Perry, Fundera, Dec. 16, 2020.

[67] For Black entrepreneurs, the wealth gap makes finding funding nearly impossible, Keenan Beasley, Fast Company Magazine, July 23, 2020.

[68] 22 Reasons Why Black Businesses Fail, A Report Brief, Dr. Brooks B. Robinson, Blackeconomics.org, Aug. 1, 2014.

[69] Policygenius survey based on nationally representative group of 1,526 adults across the U.S.een

[70] Led by Baby Boomers, divorce rates climb for America's 50+ population, By Renee Stepler, Pew Research Center, March 9, 2017.

[71] Rashawn Ray and Andrew Perry, "Why We Need Reparations for Black Americans," Big Ideas, The Brookings Institution, April 15, 2020.

Chapter Eighteen

[72] Rashawn Ray and Andrew Perry, "Why We Need Reparations for Black Americans," Big Ideas, The Brookings Institution, April 15, 2020.

[73] Kriston McIntosh, Emily Moss, Ryan Nunn, and Jay Shambaugh, Examining the Black-White Wealth Gap, Up Front, The Brookings Institution, February 27, 2020.

[74] The Ticket to Easy Street? The Financial Consequences of Winning the Lottery, Scott Hankins, Mark Hoekstra and Paige Marta Skiba, The Review of Economics and Statistics, August 1, 2011, MIT Press Direct.

[75] How Baby Bonds Could Help Close the Racial Wealth Gap, Lia Mitchell, Aron Szapiro, Morningstar Policy Research, September 2020.

Chapter Nineteen

[76] How a basic income would help close the wealth gap and give Americans needed financial security, By Amir Farokhi, MarketWatch, Outside the Box, Aug. 1, 2020.

[77] Michelle Aronowitz, former deputy general counsel for enforcement and fair housing at the Department of Housing and Urban Development, Edward Golding, MIT Golub Center, and Jung Hyan Choi, Urban Institute, The Unequal Costs of Black Homeownership, Oct. 1, 2020.

[78] U.S. Bureau of Labor Statistics, "National Business Employment Dynamics Data by Firm Size Class."

[79] "States introducing state-sponsored retirement programs continue to increase," Paychex Work, updated June 16, 2021.

About the Author

Rodney A. Brooks, a veteran newspaper journalist, writes about retirement and personal finance issues and racial and wealth and health disparities. His columns currently run in *U.S. News & World Report* and AARP's Senior Planet. He has also written columns for *The Washington Post, USA TODAY* and *TheStreet.com.*

Brooks is a contributor for National Geographic, Next Avenue, Forbes, and many others. He has also written about professional athletes and their finances for the *Undefeated*, an ESPN website.

He is co-author of *Retirement Planning Essentials: A Guide to Living Well Without Running out of Money*, published in 2018. He is also author of Is *One Million Dollars Enough: A Guide to Planning for and Living Through a Successful Retirement.* He is also a successful ghost writer, having written five other books, mostly for financial planners. He has also testified before the U.S. Senate Special Committee on Aging on the retirement crisis and wealth inequities.

Brooks was Deputy Managing Editor/Personal Finance and retirement columnist for USA TODAY, where he coordinated all personal finance on all platforms for USA TODAY. He retired in 2015 after 30 years with the Nation's Newspaper.

Previously he was assistant business editor and reporter at the *Philadelphia Inquirer*. He has also worked as a reporter or editor for *The Bulletin* in Philadelphia, the *Asheville* (N.C.) *Citizen-Times* and the *Ithaca (N.Y.) Journal.*

Born in Baltimore, Maryland and raised in Newark and Linden, New Jersey, Brooks received a B.S. degree from Cornell University and has an executive certificate in financial planning from Georgetown University. In 2021 he was inducted into the National Association of Black Journalists Hall of Fame.

Twitter: @perfiguy
Website: www.RodneyABrooks.com